Antique Trader

Salt AND Pepper Shaker

PRICE GUIDE

Mark F. Moran

©2008 Krause Publications

Published by

An Imprint of F+W Publications

700 East State Street • Iola, WI 54990-0001
715-445-2214 • 888-457-2873
www.krausebooks.com

Library of Congress Control Number: 2007934360

ISBN-13: 978-0-89689-636-9

ISBN-10: 0-89689-636-6

Designed by Marilyn McGrane and Donna Mummery

Edited by Kristine Manty

Printed in China

On the cover: Souvenir shakers from Hawaii, 4" h, 1970s, **$20+.**

Acknowledgments

Jim Langer, left, Doug Horton and their dog, Dolly, with several hundred of their shakers.

With very few exceptions, all the shakers in this book are drawn from a single collection of more than 3,000 pairs amassed by Jim Langer and Doug Horton of Minneapolis. To them, and their dog, Dolly, who liked to nap under my camera tripod, this book is respectfully and gratefully dedicated.

Thanks also to Lorraine and Leo Erickson of Iola, Wis.

Contents

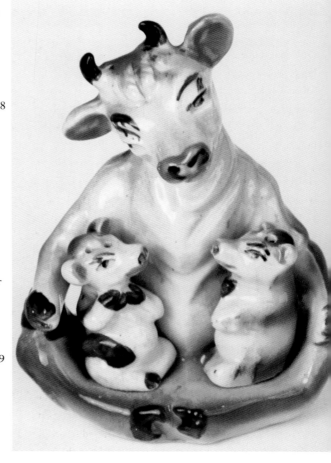

Introduction: Salt and Pepper and Their Preparation and Storage

In ancient times, salt was a precious commodity. According to Marco Polo, cakes of salt displayed a likeness of the Tibetan ruler and were used as money. In ancient Greece, slaves were traded for salt, and more than 2,000 years before the birth of Christ, the Chinese emperor levied the first known tax of any kind on salt.

In the native Japanese religion Shinto, salt is used for ritual purification of locations and people, such as in Sumo wrestling. In Aztec mythology, Huixtocihuatl was a fertility goddess who presided over salt and salt water. Reports from Onondaga, N.Y., in 1654 relate that the Onondaga Indians made salt by boiling brine from salt springs.

Egyptian art from as long ago as 1450 B.C. records the making of salt. More recent examples are drawings of a 15th-century French salt evaporation plant, a 16th-century Persian picture of a Kurdish salt merchant and a 17th-century Italian print offering instructions for distilling salt.

During the Middle Ages, when salt was a valuable commodity, it was kept on the table in elaborate metal or glass dishes as a status symbol. Being granted the favor of sharing the saltcellar of the host was seen as a sign of great respect. The social status of a person was often measured simply by judging the distance at which the guest sat from the mas-

> Pepper has also been prized for millennia. In 77 AD, Pliny the Elder, the ancient Roman nobleman, scientist and historian, wrote:
>
> "It is quite surprising that the use of pepper has come so much into fashion, seeing that in other substances which we use, it is sometimes their sweetness, and sometimes their appearance that has attracted our notice; whereas, pepper has nothing in it that can plead as a recommendation to either fruit or berry, its only desirable quality being a certain pungency; and yet it is for this that we import it all the way from India! Who was the first to make trial of it as an article of food? And who, I wonder, was the man that was not content to prepare himself by hungering only for the satisfying of a greedy appetite?"

ter's saltcellar. In the more recent past, before refrigeration, salt was the main ingredient for preserving food.

Spice mills, including those for pepper, were found in European kitchens as early as the 14th century, but the mortar and pestle used earlier for crushing pepper and salt remained a popular method for centuries after as well.

Modern salt and pepper shakers evolved from the English "muffineer" or sugar shaker. In the Victorian era, salt was kept in small individual cellars as part of a typical table setting. Covered or master saltcellars were also used.

Some early salt shakers contained a grinding mechanism to break up large salt chunks, similar to the modern pepper grinders. As salt production was refined, these grinders became obsolete.

The screw-top cap was patented by John Landis Mason in 1858 for use on fruit jars. Around 1871, when salt became more refined, some ceramic shakers were molded with perforated tops.

It's important for collectors to know that if they see an antique glass shaker with a rough or jagged top above the threaded neck, this is called the "bust-off" and is not a flaw. Some collectors grind these down, but this jagged area is a normal part of the manufacturing process, created when the shakers were taken out of the molds.

In the early 20th century, moisture-absorbing agents (magnesium carbonate) were added to salt and it was no longer sold in blocks for food use, but was finely ground. In 1924, Morton became the first company to produce iodized salt for the table to help prevent goiters, recognized as a widespread health problem in the U.S. at that time. Saltcellars finally disappeared as common table objects by the middle of the 20th century.

Rare, unique and decorative salt and pepper shakers have become such popular collector's items over the years that many shaker sets are produced for the sole purpose of being a collectible and are rarely used to hold the condiment. During their retirements, actors Glenn Ford and Bob Hope were avid collectors of vintage salt and pepper shakers. Writer and poet Dorothy Parker also had a large collection.

Salt and pepper shakers can be found in nearly every conceivable shape and size and are made in a variety of materials including wood, metal, ceramics, glass, and plastics. They are abundant, colorful, fun, span almost every theme, and best of all, they're often inexpensive. You can generally find a set of whimsical shakers for around $10, so collecting is certainly within the reach of just about anyone. Because salt and pepper shakers are easy to find and are inexpensive, some people have amassed collections numbering in the thousands.

Whether you fancy figurals, go-togethers, hangers, kissers, nesters, stackers, western styles or long-boys, you are sure to find something that catches your interest.

There is also a museum solely devoted to these shakers: The Salt and Pepper Shaker Museum, the only one of its kind, in Gatlinburg, Tenn. Each year, more than 8,000 people visit it to see the 20,000+ salt and pepper shakers featured and some of the strangest pepper mills around.

How To Use This Book

This book is divided into two broad categories: shakers listed by form and shakers listed by maker. Nearly 40 manufacturers are represented, along with forms that include advertising, assorted creatures, assorted figural, Blue Willow, characters, Christmas, clowns, ethnic, miniatures, muffineers and "nodders."

Prices

The prices in this book have been established with the help of seasoned collectors and dealers. These values reflect not only current collector trends, but also the wider economy. The adage that "an antique (or collectible) is worth what someone will pay for it" also holds true for shakers. A price guide measures value, but it also captures a moment in time, and sometimes that moment can pass very quickly.

Beginners should follow the same advice that all seasoned collectors have learned: Make mistakes and learn from them; talk with other collectors and dealers; find reputable resources (including books and Web sites), and learn to invest wisely, buying the best examples you can afford. And remember that many glass companies bought and sold molds, so one firm's early designs may show up in other colors when reused by another maker.

Resources

More information about salt and pepper shakers can be obtained from the following sources:

The National Novelty Salt and Pepper Shakers Collectors Club
http://www.saltandpepperclub.com/

The Antique and Art Glass Salt Shaker Collector's Society Inc.
http://www.antiquesaltshakers.com/

Jim Langer and Doug Horton,
612-623-0134

Reproduction Shakers

By Mark Chervenka

Shakers, like most other antiques and collectibles, have been reproduced for many years. Most reproductions are glass but new shakers are also being made of pottery and china. With few exceptions, the great majority of new glass shakers are made in new molds, not original molds. Many of the new molds—like those for Three Face, Inverted Fan and Feather and others—are intentionally designed to look like the old patterns. Careful examination, though, will find differences in pattern details and measurements between old and new.

The best defense against reproductions is a healthy skepticism. Don't assume, for example, that a particular pattern or type of material can not be reproduced. As a general rule, be suspicious if a shaker does not show any sign of normal wear consistent with age. Ask yourself if the top is the appropriate metal and finish for the age of the shaker. While replacement tops are acceptable if honestly represented on genuinely old shakers, many reproductions can be detected by their obviously flimsy and poorly made tops.

The following examples are representative of the various reproductions currently in the market. Some have only recently entered the market; others have been causing confusion since the 1970s.

Inverted Fan and Feather

Reproduction Inverted Fan and Feather shak-

The new Inverted Fan and Feather shaker, left, and original, right. The authentic shaker has four feet; the new shaker rests on a flat base. *Photo courtesy of Dr. James S. Measell.*

ers were first made from new molds in 1979 by Summit Art Glass. New shakers are quite unlike the originals. They have distinct panels around the sides and rest on a flat base. The originals have four feet and a ribbed neck. But since originals are quite scarce, many collectors and dealers have seldom seen an original. New shakers are found primarily in a custard like pale yellow glass, which may or may not be decorated with paint and/or gold trim.

Jadite

Reproductions of jadite have been produced in both China and the United States since the late 1990s. Most new jadite, including shakers, is made from new molds. New jadite shakers are very similar to vintage shapes made by original makers such as McKee, Jeannette, Anchor Hock-

New   Old

The top of the new Jeannette look-alike shaker, left, has a distinct neck between the shaker body and the beginning of the threads (arrow). The original Jeannette shaker has virtually no neck between threads and body.

This new jadite round shaker from China, left, is a close copy of an original jadite 6-oz shaker by Jeannette, right. Sizes are virtually identical, about 4-1/4" h. The key difference is the tops; see photo at top right.

Rosso square shakers, like the one at left, have a distinct neck between the shaker body and the threads. The McKee originals do not have an obvious neck.

Comparison of the new Rosso square jadite shaker to the old McKee and Jeannette shakers. The top opening in an original Jeannette, right, is 1-1/4" diameter; the opening in the other square shakers is 1-5/8" diameter. The new Rosso square shaker, left, is closest in appearance to an original McKee shaker, center. You can identify old McKee shakers by the bases and necks (see photos at right).

The original McKee square shaker, right, has a horizontal mold seam around the base; there is no similar seam on the new Rosso shaker, left. The Rosso square shakers have a stepped raised base; the McKee base is concave and domed inward.

New   Old   Old

The new Daisy and Fern opalescent shaker, left, is made from a new shape mold first used in 1979. No Victorian-era shaker in Daisy and Fern has this flat-sided shape. Middle: ca. 1890 Daisy and Fern by Northwood; right: ca. 1888 Daisy and Fern by Buckeye Glass Co.

ing and others. You need to look very carefully at molded details to separate old from new.

One of the easiest tests of age is to look for the mark of Rosso Wholesale Glass, a current distributor of reproduction glassware. Many pieces of Rosso have a molded trademark of the letter "R" in a keystone. You'll need to look close, though; on many pieces the mark is very faint and all but invisible. The best test of age for jadite shakers is to examine the molded details. The photos and captions on Page 9 discuss how to detect new jadite shakers that most closely resemble originals by Jeannette and McKee.

Opalescent Daisy and Fern

New opalescent glass Daisy shakers first began appearing in late 2004. Although honestly sold as new by a glass wholesaler, the shakers are widely offered in online auctions, malls and flea markets where the age becomes confused.

New pieces are permanently, but very faintly, marked in the base with a keystone surrounding an R, the mark of Rosso Wholesale Glass. Although this mark is potentially an important feature when dating a piece, the mark is very difficult to see. They are very weak and, unless you look carefully, are easily missed.

The shape alone is a warning sign. There are no vintage pre-1920 shakers with this flat-sided rectangular shape. The mold used for the new Daisy and Fern shaker has been used for many other new shakers from this same wholesaler including jadite.

New Daisy and Fern shakers are double or triple the thickness of vintage pre-1920 shakers with some measuring 3/16ths of an inch.

New Cherry Blossom shakers are filled with more solid glass than originals. The flared top rims on new shakers appear as four distinct tabs. Rims on original shakers are gently curved.

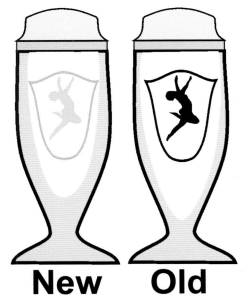

The pattern on new Cameo shakers, left, is shallow and faint. The inside cavity of new shakers has more solid glass than original shakers.

Cameo (Ballerina, Dancing Girl)

Reproductions of Cameo pattern Depression glass have been widely manufactured in the United States as well as overseas.

All originals of this pattern, also known as Ballerina and Dancing Girl, are full table-sized pieces. All the toy or child-sized pieces are recently made products. The reproduction full-sized shaker can be detected by the faint, poorly molded pattern and the extra glass near the base (see photos at left for comparison).

Cherry Blossom

Original Cherry Blossom shakers are among the rarest pieces of Depression glass, valued at more than $1,000. Although only a handful of original shakers are known, online auctions and flea markets are flooded with reproductions.

All Cherry Blossom shakers should be considered new unless careful study proves otherwise.

New shakers have much more solid glass in the bottom than the old. The flared top rim of new shakers looks like four separate squared-off tabs (see photo at top). Top rims of old shakers are gently scalloped.

Red Riding Hood

Original Little Red Riding Hood figural shakers were made by Hull in three sizes: 3-1/4, 4-1/2 and 5-1/2 inches. New shakers, attempting apparently to copy the largest original size, are being made in between the original sizes measuring about 4-7/8 inches. The filling holes in the base of originals are nearly perfectly round.

The red cape on the new Little Red Riding Hood shaker, shown here, is cold painted over the glaze. It is under the glaze in the original. Filling holes in new shakers are very rough and irregular.

Holes in the reproductions are very irregular. The red cape on the original Hull shaker is fired under the glaze; the red cape in the reproduction is cold painted over the glaze.

Pearl China shakers

Many reproductions today are copies of items originally made for utilitarian everyday use around the house, especially kitchen items like shakers. In other words, the vintage item was designed for a specific practical function. Many reproductions are designed as "collectibles" and lack the essential elements to make them function like originals. Range shakers, for example, should logically have filling holes that make practical sense. Filling holes in new Pearl range shakers are about the size of a dime; holes in originals are about 1 inch.

Most original ceramic kitchen pieces made in Japan during the 1930s, including the Pearl shakers, have at least some cold painted over glaze decoration (as opposed to under glaze decoration or paint fired-on in a kiln or oven). The total absence of cold painting or cold painting that shows no sign of normal wear, are generally warning signs of a reproduction.

Filling holes in the bases of all old shakers, right, are very nearly a perfectly smooth 1″ circle. Filling holes in the 1990s reproductions, left, are only about the size of a dime.

Pearl

These new range-size shakers are a close copy of vintage originals by Pearl China. New shakers show no trace of normal wear to cold painted decorations or gold trim.

Watt Pottery

Many shapes of Watt Pottery, including shakers, have been extensively reproduced since the mid-1990s. Almost all Watt Pottery reproduction shakers have hand-painted decorations and high-gloss glaze. Original Watt shakers in those shapes had unglazed bisque bodies, not glazed bodies.

The only glazed areas on original shakers are the brown glazed tops and the insides of the bodies which are also glazed brown. No original Watt Pottery bisque shakers were made with hand-painted patterns such as Open Apple or Autumn Foliage shown in the photo at left. Be alert, though, for new painted decorations added to genuinely old but originally never decorated bisque bodies.

Mark Chervenka is the publisher of the Internet-based Antiques and Collectors Reproduction News (www.repronews.com) and America's most recognized expert on antique fakes and reproductions. He's authored four editions of *Antique Trader Guide to Fakes & Reproductions*, as well as *Antique Trader Fakes & Forged Marks*.

A group of reproduction Watt Pottery shakers, top photo; original shakers, bottom photo. New shakers have a high-gloss glaze and hand-applied painted decorations. Original shakers have unglazed bisque bodies; no original bisque shakers have hand-painted patterns.

Shakers By Form

Collecting salt and pepper shakers is a hobby with a little something for everyone. Whether you fancy figurals, go-togethers, clowns, Christmas-related shakers, characters from cartoons, literature and pop culture, ethnic shakers, kissers, nesters or nodders, you'll quickly discover there are shakers in just about any form you can imagine.

The sections in this chapter are divided alphabetically by subject, and the shakers are also listed alphabetically within their respective sections.

ADVERTISING SHAKERS

Some the most ingenious shakers were created to advertise goods and services. This is a rich collecting area with new designs being created almost daily.

Big Boys with heart-shaped burgers, late 1980s, marked "50 years with Big Boy circa 1936," 4" h, $45-$55.

Atlas Prager Beer, 1950s, 4-3/8" h, **$35-$45.**

Borden's Elsie the Cow, 1950s, 4-1/4" h overall,
$55-$65.

Borden's Elsie the Cow with calves Larabee and Lobelia, late 1950s, 5-1/4" and 2" h, made in Japan, **$150+.** Elsie's mate is Elmer the Bull. They have four children: Beulah, Beauregard, born 1948, and twins Larabee and Lobelia, born 1957.

Budweiser Bud Man, marked "Ceramart Made in Brazil," 3-1/2" h, **$55-$65.**

Campbell's Kids, 2004, made in China, 5-1/4" and 4-3/4" h, **$20-$25.**

Budweiser Beer, 1960s, 4" h, **$45-$50.**

Campbell's Kids, contemporary, unmarked, 4-3/4" h, **$20-$25.**

Chicken of the Sea fish, 1960s, impressed mark, 3" long, **$35-$45.**

Coca-Cola bottles, contemporary, made in China, 5" h, **$15+.**

Coca-Cola delivery boy with cart, 1986, made in China, 4" and 2-1/4" h, **$20+.**

Coca-Cola polar bears, contemporary, 4" h, **$15+.**

Coke cans, contemporary, 3-1/2" h, **$10-$15.**

Coke bottle, glass and metal, salt shaker on top and pepper mill on bottom, contemporary, made in China, 7-3/4" h, **$25-$35.**

Coors steins, contemporary, unmarked, 4" h, **$20+.**

Coke machines with tray, contemporary, 7-1/2" h overall, **$25+.**

Dodgers teddy bears, 1998, made in China, 4-1/2" h, **$35-$45.**

Falstaff Beer, 1960s, 4" h, **$35-$45.**

Fingerhut tractor trailer, contemporary, made in China, 3-1/4" long overall, **$15-$20.**

Fleck's Beer, Faribault, Minn., 1950s, 4" h, **$50-$60.**

Fort Pitt Special Beer, 1950s, marked "Muth Buffalo – Pat Pend," 3" h, **$35-$45.**

G.E. electric iceboxes, molded glass, part of a set that included a refrigerator-form sugar container, 1930s; shakers only, 3-1/4" h, **$50+.**

Goetz Country Club Pilsner Beer, 1950s, 4-3/8" h, **$35-$45.**

Hamm's Bear in canoe, 1998, canoe 5" long, **$65-$75.**

Hamm's Bear in teepee, 1999, 5-1/4" h, **$75-$85.**

Hamm's Bears in Viking helmets, 2001, 5-1/2" h, **$60-$70.**

Hamm's Bear as leprechaun with pot of gold, 2004, 2-1/4" and 4-3/4" h, **$65-$75.**

Hamm's Bears with transfer decoration, this pair made in Japan, 4-1/4" h, **$65-$75.**

Hamm's Bears with transfer decoration, 1997, 4-3/4" h, **$65-$75.**

Hamm's Bears at the bar, 1997, 4-3/4" h, **$75-$85.**

Hamm's Bears with blue stripe sign, 1977, 4-3/4" h, **$75-$85.**

Hamm's Beer, 1950s, 4" h, **$35-$45.**

Holiday Hamm's Bears, contemporary, made in Japan, 3-1/4" h, **$25-$35.**

Jasper Bears, Canada (Jasper National Park, Alberta), 1960s, made in Japan, 4" h, **$35-$45.**

Joe Camel, molded resin, 1993, made in China, 4" h, **$55-$65.**

John Deere tractor and wagon, contemporary, 2-1/2" h and 4" long, **$25-$35.**

John Deere mower and rider, contemporary, 4" h overall, **$25.**

John Deere tractor, farmer and barn, contemporary, barn 3" h, tractor 3" long, **$20-$25.**

Jordan Old Style Brew Beer individual, metal, 1930s, marked "B&B St. Paul Pat Pend," 1-1/2" h, no established value.

Keebler Ernie the Elf, 1989, 4-3/8" h, **$35-$45.**

Kool cigarettes Millie and Willie, plastic, 1960s, 3-1/2" and 3-3/4" h, **$25-$35.**

Minneapolis Savings and Loan Association tree-form shakers, plastic, marked "A Good Tree To Come To For Shelter," 1980s, 3-1/2" h, **$35-$45.**

Ken-L Ration Fifi and Fido, plastic, 1960s, 3-1/2" h, **$25-$35.**

Northwest Airlines individual, 1970s, 1-1/2" h, **$15-$20.**

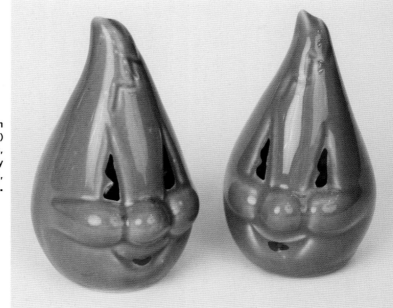

NSP (Northern States Power Co.) blue flames, 1980s, indistinctly marked, 4" h, **$55-$65.**

Phillips 66 gas pumps, plastic, 1950s, marked "Elmer Q. Lupfer – McFall, Mo.," 2-3/4" h, **$25+.**

Pillsbury Poppin' Fresh and Poppie, plastic, 1974, 4" and 3-1/2" h, **$25+.**

Pillsbury Poppin' Fresh, 1970s, 3-1/2" h, **$25+.**

Pillsbury Poppin' Fresh, impressed mark TPC, 4-1/2" h, **$15+.**

Pillsbury Poppin' Fresh and Poppie, 1988, 4" and 4-1/4" h, **$15+.**

Pillsbury Poppin' Fresh with cookies and flour sack, 1997, 3-1/2" and 4-1/8" h, **$15+.**

Pillsbury Poppin' Fresh with cookies and milk bottle, contemporary, 5" and 3-1/2" h, **$15+.**

Planters Mr. Peanut, plastic, 1960s, 4" h, **$30-$35.**

Planters
Mr. Peanut,
kitchen size,
1990, made in
Taiwan, 5" h,
$55-$65.

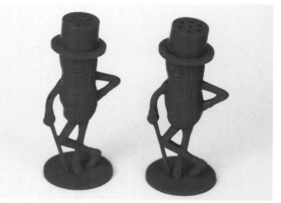

Planters Mr. Peanut, plastic, 1950s, 3-1/8" h, **$20-$25.**

RCA Victor, "His
Master's Voice,"
plastic base, Nip-
per (3" h) and
gramophone
(2-3/4" long) are
ceramic; tray
6" long,
$50-$60 set.

Rice Krispies, Pop!, marked Japan, 2-1/2" h, **$25+.**

San Francisco trolley, 1970s, 2" h, 3-1/4" long overall, **$15-$20.**

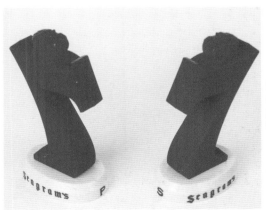

Seagram's 7 Crown whiskey, plastic, 1970s, 3-1/2" h, **$25+.**

Schlitz Export Beer, 1950s, 4-3/8" h, **$35-$45.**

Stroh's Beer Burgie!, 1998, made in Japan, 4-3/4" h, **$45-$55.**

Sunshine bakers, stamped Made in Japan, 2-3/4" h, **$50-$60.**

Tappan chefs, unmarked, 4-1/2" h, **$60-$70.**

Watkins products, contemporary, 3-1/2" and 2-3/4" h, **$10+.**

ASSORTED CREATURES

This section features a Noah's Ark of creatures, including those that swim, crawl and fly. Also see animal forms made by specific makers.

Birds hanging by tails from tree branches, late 1940s, made in Japan, 4-1/4" h overall, **$45+.**

Birds perched on branch, 1960s, made in Japan, 4-3/8" h overall, **$25-$35.**

Birds perched on flowered branch, 1960s, made in Japan, 3-1/2" h overall, **$25-$35.**

Birds with roses and gold trim, contemporary, made in China, 2-1/2" h, **$20+.**

Bluebirds in flowered straw hats, 1960s, made in Japan by Lefton, 3-1/2" h, $35-$45.

Bluebirds wearing flower hats, 1960s, made in Japan, 3-1/2" and 3-3/4" h, $25-$35.

Bluebirds in flowered straw hats, 1960s, made in Japan by Lefton, 3-1/2" h, $35-$45.

Bluebirds with rhinestone eyes, 1960s, made in Japan, 3" h, $35+.

Blue Jays, 1950s, made in Japan, 3-1/4" and 3" h, **$25+.**

Cockatiels, 1950s, made in Japan, 3" and 3-1/2" h, **$25+.**

Crows in hats, 1950s, ink-stamped Japan, 2-1/2" h, **$40-$50.**

Chicks emerging from eggs, 1950s, made in Japan, 3" h, **$20+.**

Blue chicks with feathers and rhinestones, 1950s, 3″ h without feathers, **$35-$45.**

Flowered chicks, contemporary, unmarked, 3″ h, **$20+.**

Chicks with rhinestone eyes, 1960s, made in Japan, 3″ h, **$35+.**

Happy chicks, 1980s, 3″ h, **$20+.**

Luster-ware egg-shaped chicks with goose in shell holder, 1930s, made in Japan, 2-3/4″ h overall, **$25-$30.**

Twin chicks emerging from egg, 1950s, made in Japan, 5-1/4″ w, **$30+.**

Delft blue hens on flower baskets, contemporary, 3-1/2″ h, **$15+.**

Hen and chick emerging from egg, 1950s, made in Japan, 1-1/4″ and 2-3/4″ h, **$25-$35.**

Hen and rooster, air-brushed, 1970s, 4-3/4" and 5" h, **$35-$45.**

Hen and rooster, 1960s, made in Japan, 3-1/2" and 5" h, **$30-$40.**

Hen and rooster, 1960s, made in Japan, 3-3/4" and 4" h, **$30-$40.**

Hen and rooster, 1950s, made in Japan, 2-3/4" and 4" h, **$20+.**

Hen and rooster, 1950s, made in Japan, 2-3/4" and 3-3/4" h, **$20+.**

Hen and rooster, 1950s, made in Japan, 3-1/2" and 4-1/4" h, **$25+.**

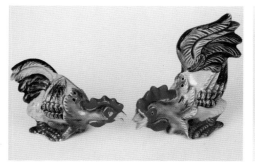

Fighting hen and rooster, 1960s, made in Japan, 2-3/4" and 4" h, **$20+.**

Rooster and hen, 1980s, 4-3/4" and 3-3/4" h, **$20+.**

Glass and metal rooster and hen, 1970s (?), maker unknown, 4" h, **$25-$35.**

Flowered ducks, contemporary, unmarked, 3" long, **$20+.**

Ducks in hat and apron, 1980s, unmarked, 3-1/4" and 3" h, **$25+.**

Flowered ducks with books and gold trim, 1970s, made in Japan, 3-1/2" and 3-3/4" h, **$25+.**

Formal ducks, 1970s, made in Japan, 5-1/4" h, **$25-$30.**

Flowered ducklings with gold trim, 1970s, made in Japan, 3" h, **$20+.**

Large-bill ducklings, 1940s, marked Germany, 3" h, **$45-$55.**

Flamingos, 1980s, unmarked, 4" and 2-3/4" h, **$20+.**

Tall mother geese in bonnets, 1950s, made in Japan, 8-1/4" h, **$25-$35.**

Ruffed grouse, 1950s, made in Japan, 2-3/4" and 3-1/8" h, **$30+.**

Herons, 1960s, made in Japan, 4" h, **$25-$35.**

Orioles, 1950s, made in Japan, 3-1/8" h, **$30+.**

Owls with rhinestone eyes, 1970s, made in Japan by Enesco, 3" h, **$25-$35.**

Cartoon owls, 1960s, unmarked, 3" and 3-1/4" h, **$25+.**

Portly owls in waistcoats, 1940s, marked Germany, 3" h, **$45-$55.**

The Owl and the Pussycat, 1980, Fitz & Floyd, came with boat, 2-1/2" h; **$15+** as is; with boat, **$30+.**

Wise owls with mortarboards and rhinestone eyes, 1960s, made in Japan by Lefton, round wooden bases a later addition, 3-3/4" h, **$30.**

Parakeets, 1960s, made in Japan, 2-1/2" and 3-1/2" long, **$35+.**

Parrots, 1950s, made in Japan, 3-1/2" h, **$25+.**

Exotic pheasants, 1960s, unmarked, 4" long, **$30+.**

Pigeons, bone china, 1970s (?), made in Japan, 2-3/4" long, **$15+.**

Pileated woodpeckers, 1950s, unmarked, 3" h, **$20+.**

Puffins, contemporary, indistinct mark, 3" h, **$30+.**

Quail, 1950s, made in Japan, 2-3/4" and 3-1/4" h, **$20+.**

Swans with gold trim, early 1970s, made in Japan, 2-3/8" h, **$20+.**

Turkey tom and hen, 1950s, made in Japan, 3-3/4" and 3-1/4" h, **$25+.**

Turkey tom and hen, 1960s, made in Japan, 3-1/2" and 3-1/4" h, **$25+.**

Waxwings, 1950s, made in Japan, 2-3/4" and 3" h, **$25+.**

Wood ducks, late 1950s, made in Japan, 2-3/4" and 4" h, **$30+.**

Woodpecker and cardinal on flowered branch with gold trim, 1960s, made in Japan, 3-1/2" h overall, **$25-$35.**

Black cats with rhinestone eyes, 1960s, made in Japan, 3-7/8" h, **$30-$35.**

Boy and girl cats with rhinestone eyes, 1950s, made in Japan, 3" h, **$25-$35.**

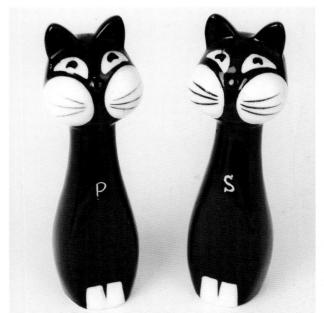

Cats, bisque, contemporary, made in China, 3-1/4" h and 3-1/2" long, **$15-$20.**

Tall black cats, 1960s, made in Japan, 6-3/4" h, **$40-$50.**

Cats, 1970s,
unmarked, 3″ h
and long,
$20-$25.

Cats in flowered
hats, 1950s, made
in Japan by Lefton,
3″ h, **$30+.**

Cats on plaid pillows, late 1950s, 3-1/2″ h,
$15-$20.

Cats in striped shirts, 1960s, made in Japan, 5″ h,
$15-$20.

Floral cats, 1960s, made in Japan, 4-1/2" h and 4" long, **$20-$25.**

Flower cats, air-brush, 1950s, 3" h, **$15-$20.**

Fluffy cats, bone china, 1980s, unmarked, 2-1/4" h and long, **$20-$25.**

Pink cats decorated with flowers and rhinestones, 1950s, made in Japan, 4" h, **$30.**

Playful cats, 1960s, with decal, Souvenir of Greenville, Texas, made in Japan, 3-1/4" h and long, **$20-$25.**

Quizzical cats, 1980s (?), 2-1/2" h, **$10-$15.**   Siamese cats, 1970s, unmarked, 4" h, **$20-$25.**

Stretch cats with rhinestone eyes, 1950s, made in Japan, 10-1/2" long, **$35-$40.**

Striped cats, 1960s, made in Japan, 3-3/4" h and long, **$25-$30.**

Striped cats with ball, 1950s, made in Japan, 3-1/2" h, **$25-$30.**

Suspicious cats, 1960s, made in Japan, 3-1/4" h, **$25.**

White cats, bisque, age unknown, unmarked, 1-3/4" h and long, **$10-$15.**

Big-eyed kittens, 1960s, made by Lefton in Japan, 3-1/4" h, **$20-$25.**

Kittens with fabric bows, late 1950s, 3-1/8" h and 2-1/2" long, **$20-$25.**

Kittens on pillows, 1950s, made in Japan, 3-1/2" and 3" h, **$25-$35.**

Kittens in teapots, 1960s, made in Japan, 2-3/4" h, **$20-$25.**

Alaskan malamutes,
1960s, unmarked,
3" h, **$20-$25.**

Bassett hounds,
1960s, made in
Japan by Norcest,
3-1/8" and
3-5/8" h, **$20+.**

Basset hound pup-
pies, 1960s, made
in Japan, 4" and 3"
long, **$25-$30.**

Basset hound pup-
pies, 1960s, made
in Japan, 2-3/4" h
and 3-1/2" long,
$20-$25.

Bonzo dogs, 1970s, made in Japan, 3-1/8" h, **$20-$25.**

Tall beagles, 1950s, made in Japan by Norcrest, 6-3/4" h, **$25-$35.**

Boston terriers, 1960s, made in Japan, 3" and 2-3/4" h, **$20-$25.**

Boston terriers, 1960s, made in Japan, 3-1/2" h and long, **$25-$35.**

Boxer puppies, 1970s, unmarked, 2" h, **$20.**

Playful Boxer puppies, 1960s, 3" h and 3-1/4" long, **$25+.**

Bulldog in top hat and laughing beagle with rhinestone monocles, 1960s-70s, 3-1/4" h, **$20-$30.**

Bulldog puppies in barrels, 1960s, made in Japan, 3" h, **$20-$25.**

Chihuahuas, 1960s, made in Japan, 4" h and 4-1/2" long, **$20-$25.**

Chihuahuas, 1970s, unmarked, 3-3/8" h, **$25-$30.**

Cocker spaniels, 1950s, unmarked, 4" h, **$25-$30.**

Collies, 1960s, made in Japan, 4-1/2" long, **$20-$25.**

Dachshunds, 1960s, made in Japan, 4" and 3-1/2" long, **$25-$30.**

Dalmatians, 1960s, made in Japan, 3-1/4" long, **$20-$25.**

Dachshunds, 1940s, Occupied Japan, 3-3/4" h, **$30-$35.**

Stretch dachshund, one piece with salt at one end and pepper at other, with decal for Hills of Indiana, 1950s, made in Japan, 10" long, **$35-$45.**

Dalmatians, 1960s, unmarked, 3-1/2" h and 4-1/2" long, **$20-$25.**

Doberman Pinschers, 1980s, made in Japan, 4-1/2" long and 4" h, **$25-$30.**

English Springer spaniels, 1950s, unmarked, 3" h, **$20-$25.**

English Springer spaniels, 1960s, made in Japan, 4-1/2" long and 3-1/4" h, **$25-$30.**

Old English
sheepdogs,
1980s,
2-3/4" h,
$25-$30.

Poodle chefs, 1950s, made in Japan, 3-1/2" h,
$20-$25.

Formal poodle couple, 1960s, made in Japan,
3-1/2" h, **$20-$25.**

Poodle couple, bone china, age unknown, 2-3/4"
and 2-1/2" h, **$20.**

Poodle puppies with bows, late 1950s, made in Japan, 4" h, **$20-$25.**

Poodle couple, hand painted, 1960s, made in Japan, 4-1/2" and 3-3/4" h, **$20-$25.**

Staffordshire-style poodles, 1960s (?), 1-3/4" h, **$15-$20.**

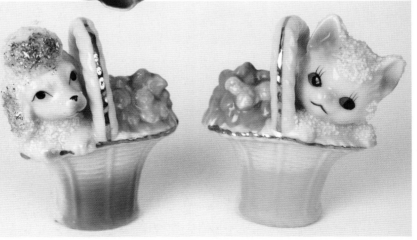

Poodle puppy and kitten in flower baskets, late 1950s, made in Japan, 3-1/2" h, **$25-$35.**

Pug puppies, contemporary, made in China, 3-1/2" long and h, **$15.**

Scotties, age unknown, unmarked, 2-1/8" h, **$15-$20.**

Scottie puppies, 1960s-70s, made in Japan, 1-3/4" h, **$10-$15.**

Scotties, crystal and red glass, 1950s, 2-1/4" h, **$35-$45.**

Scottie puppies in plaid caps, 1940s, Occupied Japan, 2-3/4" h, **$25-$35.**

Sad Scotties, 1950s, with threaded ceramic stoppers, made in Japan, 3-3/4" h, **$25-$30.**

Shih Tzu puppies (?), 1960s-70s, made in Japan, 1-3/4" h, **$15-$20.**

Spaniels doing tricks, 1950s, made in Japan, 3-3/4" and 4" h, **$35-$45.**

Spaniel and poodle with rhinestone monocles, 1960s, maker unknown, 3-1/4" h, **$20+.**

Souvenir spaniels (Las Vegas?), marked "America's Marriage Place," 1960s, 3-1/2" h, **$25-$30.**

Puppies, 1960s, unmarked, 3-3/4" h, **$15-$20.**

Wire-haired fox terriers, 1950s, made in Japan, 2-5/8" h, **$20-$25.**

Playful puppies, 1950s, made in Japan, 2-3/4" h, **$25-$30.**

Sad puppies, 1960s, made in Japan, 4" h, **$25-$30.**

Clowning dogs, 1950s, made in Japan, 4-3/8" and 4-1/4" h, **$35-$45.**

Dog couple with bones, 1987, 3-1/2" h, **$20-$25.**

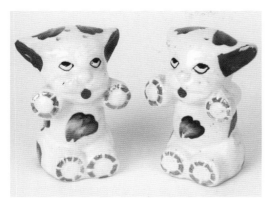

Funny dogs, hand painted with gold trim, 1950s, 2-3/4" h, **$20-$25.**

Formal dogs, late 1950s, made in Japan, 4" h, **$30+.**

Happy dogs, 1960s, made in Japan, 3-1/4" h, **$20-$25.**

Stretch dogs, 1960s, made in Japan, 4-1/2" long, **$20-$25.**

Yellow dogs in tuxedoes, late 1940s, made in Japan, 2-3/4" h, **$25+.**

Bear huggers, 1950s, made in Germany, 3-3/4" h, **$45-$55.**

Playful bear cubs, one sits on the other, 1950s, made in Japan, 3" and 2-3/4" h, **$25+.**

Glass and metal dog and cat, 1920s, maker unknown, 2-3/4 h, **$75-$100.**

Bison, 1960s, souvenir of Memphis, Tenn., made in Japan, 4" long, **$30+.**

Wild boars, bone china, 1970s, made in Japan, 2-1/2" long, **$20-$30.**

Angus bulls, 1960s, made in Japan, 4" long, **$30+.**

Brahma bulls, 1960s, unmarked, 4" long, **$25-$35.**

Brahma bulls, 1960s, made in Japan, 4" long, **$25-$35.**

Brahma bulls, 1960s, Made in Japan by Wales, 4" long, **$25-$35.**

Hereford bulls, 1960s, souvenir of Sirloin Club, South St. Paul, made in Japan, 4" long, **$25-$35.**

Bulls with handles, 1950s, made in Japan, 2-1/2" h, **$25+.**

Charging bulls, 1970s, unmarked, 5" long, **$25+.**

African cattle, bone china, 1970s, made in Japan, 2-1/2" and 3" long, **$25+.**

Longhorn cattle, 1960s, made in Japan, 4" long, **$25-$35.**

Cow and bull, 1960s, made in Japan, 3" long, **$35-$45.**

Cow and bull with roses and gold trim, 1960s, made in Japan, 3-3/4" and 3" h, **$30+.**

Playful cow and bull, 1950s, made in Japan, 3-5/8" and 3" h, **$20+.**

Bunny huggers, 1960s, made in Japan, 3-1/2" and 3-1/4" h, **$25+.**

Tall brown cows, 1960s, made in Japan, 7" h, **$25-$35.**

Blue bunnies with gold trim, age unknown, unmarked, 3" h, **$20+.**

Flower buds with butterflies on handled tray, late 1940s, Occupied Japan, 3-1/2" h overall, **$35-$45.**

Girl bunnies in short jackets, 1980s, made in Japan, 2-3/4" h, **$20+.**

Tall gray deer, 1970s, unmarked, 10" h, **$25-$35.**

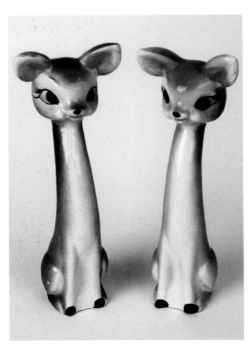

Stretch fawns, 1960s, made in Japan, 8" h, **$25-$35.**

Playful donkeys, 1960s, made in Japan by Lefton, 4" h, **$25-$35.**

Playful donkeys, 1960s, made in Japan, 3-1/2" and 3-1/4" h, **$20+.**

Dolphins, 1960s, made in Japan, 5-1/2" long, **$25-$35.**

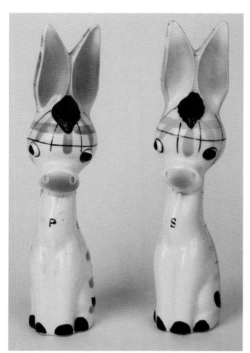

Elephants, 1950s, unmarked, 4" long, **$20+.**

Tall plaid donkeys, 1950s, made in Japan, 7" h, **$25-$35.**

Elephant and duck, 1930s, made in Japan, 3-1/4" and 3-1/2" h, **$35-$45.**

Elephant couple, 1950s, similar to Ceramic Arts Studio, made in Japan, 3-1/2" and 4" h, **$20+.**

Elephants with hair, 1960s, made in Japan, 4-1/2" h, **$20+.**

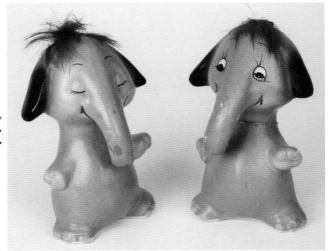

Portly elephants in waistcoats, 1940s, 3" h, marked Germany, **$45-$55.**

Wedding elephants, 1960s, made in Japan, 2-1/2" h, **$20+.**

Giraffes, 1960s, made in Japan, 3-3/4" h, **$25-$35.**

Happy hippopotami, 1950s, made in Japan, 3-1/2" long, **$20+.**

Horses in collars on tray, 1950s, made in Japan, 3" h overall, tray 4" wide, **$25+.**

Rearing horses, 1960s, made in Japan, 4-1/2" h, **$25+.**

Palomino horse heads, 1960s, souvenir of Niagara Falls, Canada, made in Japan, 3" h, **$25+.**

Rearing horses, 1970s, made in Japan, 4-1/2" h, **$25+.**

Koala bears and joeys hanging from tree branches, 1950s, made in Japan, 4-1/4" h overall, **$45+.**

Leopards, 1960s, unmarked, 5" and 3-3/4" long, **$25-$35.**

Lions, 1960s, made in Japan, 4-1/2" and 3-3/4" long, **$25-$35.**

Lions, 1960s, made in Japan, 5" long, **$25-$35.**

Lion and lioness, bone china, 1970s, convention souvenir, made in Japan, 3 and 2-1/2" long, **$15-$20.**

Stately lion heads, 1960s, made in Japan, 3-1/2" h, **$20-$25.**

Lobsters, 1940s, 3-1/2" h, **$45+.**

Lobsters, 1970s, 4-1/2" long, **$25+.**

Lobster claws, 1960s, 4-1/4" h, **$25+.**

Mice, 1960s, unmarked, 3" h, **$20+.**

Girl manta rays, 1960s, made in Japan, 4" long, **$20-$25.**

Mice with pipes and rhinestone monocles, 1950s-60s, made in Japan, 3-1/4" h, **$30-$40.**

Mr. and Mrs. Mouse, 1950s, made in Japan, 3-1/2" and 3-1/4" h, **$20+.**

Blue pigs with rhinestone eyes, 1960s, 3-3/4" h, **$25-$35.**

Brown mice with rhinestone eyes, 1950s, made in Japan by Norcrest, 3-5/8" h, **$50.**

Pig combo, 1940s, made in Germany, 2-1/2" h and wide, **$35-$45.**

Pig serenade, 1980s, maker unknown, 4" h, **$25+.**

Pigs, 1970s, unmarked, 4" long, **$20+.**

Pigs in red hats, 1970s, unmarked, 3" long, **$20+.**

Delft rabbits, contemporary, 2-1/4" long, **$15+.**

Formal rabbits, 1960s, made in Japan, 3-1/8" and 3-3/8" h, **$20+.**

Flirting rabbits, 1960s, made in Japan, 4" h, **$25+.**

Kissing rabbits with carrots, 1979, 3-7/8" and 4" h, **$25+.**

Mr. and Mrs. Rabbit, late 1950s, made in Japan, 3-3/4" h, **$25+.**

Mother rabbits with garden harvest, age unknown, made in Japan, 4" h, **$20+.**

Playful rabbits, 1960s, maker unknown, 3-1/2" h and long, **$20+.**

Rabbits with carrots and warning signs, 1980s (?), made in Japan, 3-1/4" h, **$15+.**

Rabbits in flower hats with gold trim, 1960s, made in Japan, 3-3/8" h, **$25+.**

Scary red rabbits, early 1950s, made in Japan, 3" h, **$30+.**

Reserved rabbits, 1980s, maker unknown, 3-3/4" h, **$20+.**

Spooky yellow rabbits in ruffled collars, 1950s, made in Japan, 2-3/4" h, **$25+.**

White rabbits with blue eyes, late 1960s, made in Japan, 4" and 3-1/2" h, **$25+.**

White rabbits with pink eyes, early 1950s, made in Japan, 3" h, **$20+.**

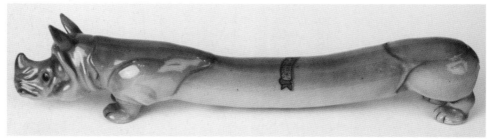

Stretch rhinoceros, one piece with salt at one end and pepper at other, souvenir of Virginia Beach, Va., 1950s, made in Japan, 10-1/2" long, **$35-$45.**

Seahorses with transfer floral decoration, 1950s, 4-1/4" h, **$35-$40.**

Skunk couple, 1960s, made in Japan, 2-1/4" and 2-3/4" h, **$30+.**

Skunk couple with flowers, 1960s, made in Japan, 3" h, **$20+.**

Squirrels with acorns and rhinestone eyes, 1960s, maker unknown, 3-3/8" h, **$20-$30.**

Tigers, 1960s, made in Japan, 4" and 4-1/2" long, **$25+.**

Tigers with whiskers, 1960s, 3-1/2" h, **$20-$25.**

Unicorns with gold trim, 1970s, made in Taiwan, 3-1/2" h, **$20+.**

Stretch zebra, one piece with salt at one end and pepper at other, 1950s, made in Japan, 10-1/4" long, **$35-$45.**

Zebras, 1960s, made in Japan, 3-1/2" h, **$20+.**

Barracuda, 1950s, made in Japan, 6" long, **$25+.**

Bass, 1950s, made in Japan, 4-1/2" long, **$25+.**

Bass, 1950s, made in Japan, 3-1/2" long, **$20+.**

Bass, 1960s, made in Japan, 4-1/2" long, **$25+.**

Small-mouth black bass, 1960s, made in Japan, 4-1/2" long, **$30+.**

Blowfish, 1960s, made in Japan, 3-1/4" long, **$25+.**

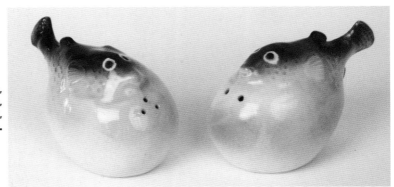

Koi, 1950s, made in Japan, 3-3/8" long, **$15+.**

Crayfish, age unknown, 3-1/2" long, **$20+.**

Perch, late 1950s, made in Japan, 4-1/2" long, **$25+.**

Northern Pike, 1960s, made in Japan, 5-1/2" long, **$30+.**

Sunfish, 1960s, made in Japan, 3-1/4" and 4" h, **$30+.**

Swordfish, 1950s, made in Japan, 4-1/4" h, **$35-$45.**

Swordfish, 1960s,
made in Japan,
5" long,
$45-$55.

Tiger shark, 1960s,
made in Japan,
5-3/4" long,
$25+.

Tropical fish,
1980s, 4-1/4"
long, **$25+.**

Tropical fish,
1950s, made in
Japan, 2" h,
$15+.

Tropical fish, 1950s, made in Japan, 3-3/4" long, **$25+.**

Tropical fish, 1960s, souvenir of Marquette, Mich., made in Japan, 3" h, **$25-$35.**

Tropical fish, 1960s, made in Japan, 3-1/2" h, **$30-$40.**

Tropical fish, 1960s, made in Japan, 3-1/4" h, **$25-$35.**

Tropical fish, 1960s, made in Japan, 2-3/4" h, **$25-$35.**

Tropical fish, 1960s, made in Japan, 3-1/4" h, **$25+.**

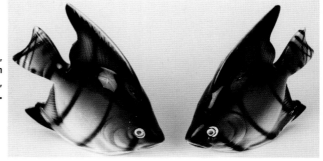

Tropical fish, 1960s, made in Japan, 3-1/2" h, **$25-$35.**

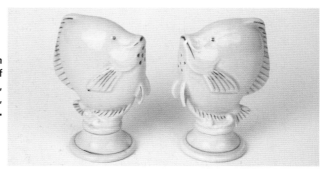

Tropical fish with screw-off bases, 1960s, made in Japan, 3-5/8" h, **$30+.**

Tropical fish,
1950s, made in
Japan, 2-3/4" h,
$30+.

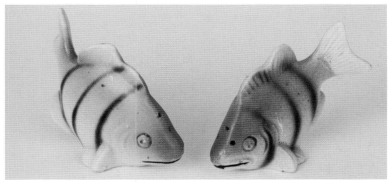

Tropical fish,
1960s, made in
Japan, 4" long,
$25+.

Tropical fish,
1960s, made in
Japan, 3-1/2" h,
$25+.

Tropical fish,
1950s, made in
Japan, 3" h,
$20+.

Tropical fish,
1960s, made in
Japan, 2-3/4" h,
$25+.

Tropical fish, late
1950s, made in
Japan, 3" h,
$25+.

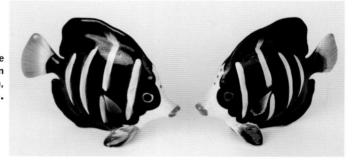

Tropical fish,
1960s, made in
Japan, 2-3/4" h,
$25+.

Tropical fish,
1950s, made in
Japan, 3-3/8" h,
$25+.

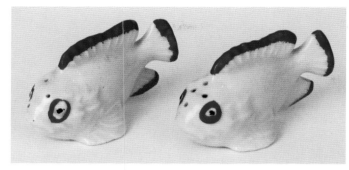

Tropical fish, contemporary, 2-1/2" long, **$10+.**

Three tropical fish, bone china, contemporary, 2-5/8" h, **$20+.**

Tropical fish, bone china, contemporary, 3 h, **$20+.**

Tropical fish, 1960s, made in Japan, 3-3/4" and 4" h, **$20+.**

Tropical fish, 1950s, made in Japan, 2-3/4" h, **$20+.**

Tropical fish, 1960s, made in Japan, 3" long, **$20+.**

Tropical fish, 1960s, souvenir of Manistique, Mich., made in Japan, 5" long, **$25+.**

Tropical fish with rhinestone eyes, 1950s, made in Japan, 3-1/2" h, **$45-$40.**

Trout, 1960s, made in Japan, 5" long, **$25+.**

Trout, 1950s, made in Japan, 3-1/2" long, **$25+.**

Trout, 1960s, made in Japan, 7" long, **$25+.**

Trout, 1970s, made in the Philippines, 4" long, **$25+.**

Tropical fish with rhinestone eyes, souvenir of Multnomah Falls, Ore., 1960s, made in Japan, 3" h, **$30-$40.**

Trout, 1960s, marked "Missouri the Show-Me State," made in Japan, 5" long, **$25+.**

Boy and girl fish, 1950s, made in Japan, 3" long, **$25+.**

Boy and girl flirting fish, 1950s, made in Japan, 4" h, **$25+.**

Flirting girl fish, 1960s, made in Japan, 3-1/4" h, **$25+.**

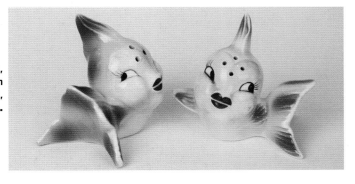

Mr. and Mrs. Fish in hats, 1950s, made in Japan, 2-1/2" and 3" h,
$25+.

Game fish, 1960s, made in Japan, 5" long, **$25+.**

Luster-ware fish, 1950s,
unmarked, 4-1/4" h, **$20+.**

"Tell it to the fin" fish in hats, one piece, 1950s, made in Japan,
4" h, **$35+.**

ASSORTED FIGURAL SHAKERS

Shakers in this section depict people, beings with human form or inanimate objects with human characteristics, and are the products of many makers.

This category includes "Naughties," usually anatomically incorrect women in various poses. Also see figural forms made by specific makers.

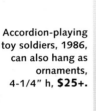

Accordion-playing toy soldiers, 1986, can also hang as ornaments, 4-1/4" h, **$25+.**

Angel with blue wings, 1940s, marked Rossware, 3-3/4" h, **$65-$75.**

Angel with gold trim, 1940s, marked Rossware, 3-3/4" h, **$65-$75.**

Little angels with gold trim, 1960s, made in Japan by Lefton, 4-1/4" and 4" h, **$25-$35.**

Formal boy in top hat, 1940s, made in Japan, 4-3/4" h overall, **$45-$55.**

Frowning boys with pipes in plaid caps, 1940s, made in Germany, 3-1/2" and 3-1/8" h, **$55-$65.**

Boy and girl riding swans, 1950s, made in Japan, 3" h, **$25+.**

Nude women, 1950s,
unmarked, 3-3/4" h,
$65-$75.

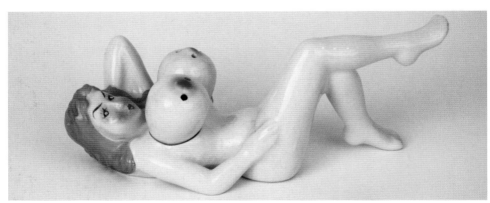

Busty woman, 1950s, made in Japan, 7" long, **$75-$85.**

Glass and metal chefs, 1970s (?), maker unknown,
3-1/4" h, **$25-$35.**

Children with petal collars, late 1950s, unmarked,
2-1/2" h, **$25+.**

Couple in 18th-century dress with gold trim, 1950s, made in Japan, 3-3/4" and 3-7/8" h, **$25+.**

Cowboy, souvenir of Eden Valley, Minn., 1960s, made in Japan, 3-3/4" h overall, **$45-$55.**

Sexy black and red girl devils, 1950s, made in Japan, 4-3/4" h, **$35-$45.**

Egghead couple with rhinestone eyes, 1950s, made in Japan, 3-1/4" h, **$30-$40.**

Four-eyed rustic couple, 1950s, made by Enesco in Japan, 3-1/2" h, **$20-$25.**

Portly gentlemen with pipes and canes, 1930s, made in Germany, 3-3/8" h, **$45-$55.**

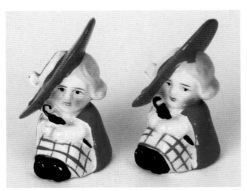

Girls in big hats with umbrellas, 1940s, made in Japan, 3-1/2" h, **$25-$35.**

Girls in hats riding tropical fish, 1930s, made in Japan, 2-3/4" h, **$25-$35.**

Lady riding alligator, 1950s, made in Japan, 4-1/4" h overall, 5" long, **$60.**

Metropolitan Museum of Art satin and crystal footed shakers in a three-face pattern, contemporary, based on a Duncan & Miller mold, marked MMA, 3-1/4" h, **$45-$55.**

Mr. and Mrs. Crazy Big-Head, late 1960s, unmarked, 4-3/4" h, **$25+.**

Pilgrim women, 1950s, made in Japan, 3-1/4" h, **$20+.**

Boy and girl pixies (?), with gold trim, 1960s, made in Japan, 3-3/4" h, **$20+.**

Pixie heads, 1960s (?), unmarked, 3-1/4" h, **$25-$35.**

Pixie heads, 1960s, unmarked, 3-3/4" h, **$40-$50.**

unning spoon and fork, 1960s, made in Japan,
-1/4" h, **$20.**

Running spoon and fork, 1960s, made in Japan,
4-1/4" and 4-1/2" h, **$20.**

tisque arguing couple, 1950s, made in Japan,
-3/4" h, **$55-$65.**

Showering couple, made as two pieces but sold
attached, 1960s, made in Japan, 5" h, **$40+.**

Southern belles in hoop skirts, early 1950s, souvenir of Des Moines, Iowa, made in Japan, 3" h, **$20-$25.**

Spice of Life, 1950s, made in Taiwan, 6" long, **$55-$65.**

Tired housewives, 1960s, unmarked, 5" h, **$35-$45.**

Toby couple, 1960s, made in Japan, 2-3/4" h, **$20+.**

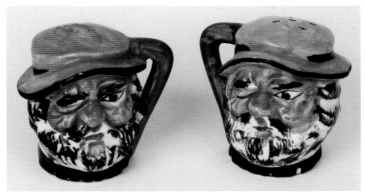

Toby bearded men (hobos?), 1960s, made in Japan, 2-1/2" h, **$20+.**

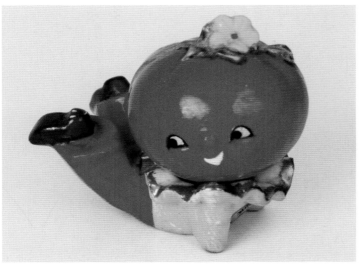

Tomato-head boy, 1940s, made in Japan, 2-1/2" h overall, **$45+.**

Black and white Venus de Milo, plastic, 1960s, 4" h, **$15-$25.**

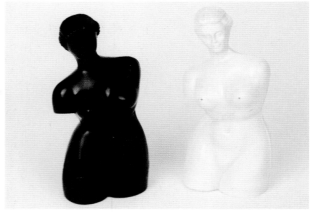

Victorian children, with threaded ceramic stoppers, 1930s, made in Japan, 3-1/8" and 3-1/4" h, **$35-$45.**

Winter children in long coats, 1940s, Occupied Japan, 3-1/4" h, **$25-$35.**

BLUE WILLOW

The Blue Willow design may be linked to an ancient Chinese tale of two star-crossed lovers. The pattern was popularized by Josiah Spode in the late 18th century and produced by hundreds of makers over the years.

Bulbous, 1950s, 3-1/2" h, **$40-$50.**

Bulbous, contemporary, 2-3/4" h, **$20+.**

Coffeepot, contemporary, 2-3/4" h, **$20+.**

Cows, contemporary, 2-3/4" h, **$20+.**

Cruet form with tray, 1950s, unmarked; tray, 5-1/2" long; shakers, 3-1/2" h, **$55-$65.**

Figural, contemporary, 4" h, **$20+.**

Kitchen, contemporary,
3-7/8" h, **$25-$35.**

Muffineer-form, 1940s,
ink-stamped Japan,
4-1/2" h, **$175.**

Obelisk, 1950s, made
in Japan, 3-3/8" h,
$35-$45.

CHARACTER SHAKERS

The shakers pictured here are drawn from literature, cartoons and pop culture.

Barber shaving a pig, 1950s, made in Japan, 2-1/2" and 3-3/4" h, **$20+.** From the nursery rhyme: "Barber, barber, shave a pig! How many hairs to make a wig? Four and twenty, that's enough! Give the barber a pinch of snuff."

The Big Bad Wolf and Little Red Riding Hood, 1950s, unmarked, 3-1/4" h, **$25.**

Cowboys Bugs Bunny and Daffy Duck, 1993, 5-3/8" and 5" h, **$55-$65.**

Bugs Bunny in leather jacket and Honey Bunny in poodle skirt, 1994, made in China, 5-3/4" h, **$35-$45.**

Paul Bunyan and Babe the Blue Ox, 1960s, origin unknown, 5-1/4" and 3" h, **$25+.**

Bugs Bunny and Elmer Fudd, 2000, 5-3/8" and 5" h, **$45-$55.**

Crows in hats ("Dumbo" characters?), 1960s, made in Japan, 4-1/4" h, **$35-$45.**

Dickensian characters, Bumble and Mrs. Gamp, 1940s, marked Germany, 3" h, **$65-$75** if perfect. Bumble is the Beadle in the workhouse depicted in *Oliver Twist*. Mrs. Gamp is a nurse in *Martin Chuzzlewit*.

Huck Finn and Becky, 1940s, marked Pat Pending 392, 4" h, **$125-$150.**

Humpty Dumpty, 1950s, unmarked, 2-1/2" h, **$85-$100.**

Humpty Dumpty sitting on wall, 1940s, unmarked, 3-1/2" h, **$65-$75.**

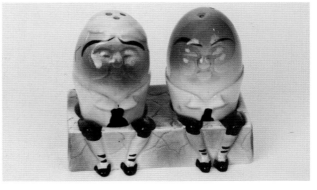

Laughing Felix the Cat, contemporary, marked "Clay Art 1997," 5" h and 5" long, **$35+.**

Little Bo Peep and her sheep, 1950s, made in Japan, 3" h, **$25.**

Waving Mickey Mouse in car, 1990s, 3-1/4" h overall, **$45-$55.**

Mickey Mouse in easy chair, 1990s, 3-1/4" h overall, **$45-$55.**

Mickey and Minnie Mouse heads, 2000, 3-1/4" and 3-3/8" h, **$45-$55.**

Seated Minnie and Mickey Mouse, 1990s, 3" and 3-3/8" h, **$45-$55.**

Mother Goose and boy riding goose, 1950s, made in Japan, 3" and 4" h, **$20+.**

Old King Cole and his Fiddler, 1950s, made in Japan, 3-1/4" h, **$20+.**

Olive Oyl and Popeye, 1980, made in Korea, 7" and 7-1/2" h, **$85-$100.**

Pluto balancing teacup and with bones, 1950s, made in Japan, 3-3/8" long and h, **$25-$30.**

Black and white Elvis with silver and gold trim, late 1980s (?), unmarked, 5-1/4" h, **$65-$75.**

Smokey Bear, 1960s, made in Japan, 4" h, **$65-$75.**

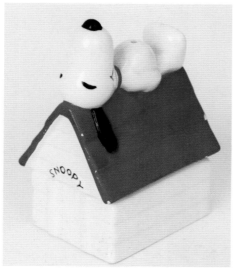

Snoopy on doghouse, Snoopy and roof are one piece, 1980s, 4-1/2" h overall, **$35-$45.**

Sylvester and Tweety Bird on birdcage with mallet, 1993, 4-1/2" h, **$45-$55.**

Sylvester and Tweety Bird in nest, 1990s, unmarked, 4-1/2" and 2" h, **$45-$55.**

Tasmanian Devil baseball players, 1990s, 4-1/4" h, $45-$55.

Wiley Coyote and Roadrunner, 1993, 5-3/4" and 5" h, **$35-$45.**

Ziggy and his dog, Fuzz, 1979 copyright, made in Japan, 2-1/4" and 3" h, **$25+.**

CHRISTMAS SHAKERS

Christmas-themed salt and pepper shakers add a festive touch to your holiday dinner table.

Birds with holly hats, 1960s, made in Japan, 3-1/4" h, **$25-$35.**

Christmas angels, one with wreath, 1960s, made in Japan, 2-1/2" h, **$20+.**

Sleepy Christmas angels, 1960s, made in Japan, 2-3/4" h, **$25+.**

Christmas angels with floral trim, 1950s, made in Japan, 3-3/4" h, **$35+.**

Christmas girls with bell and candy cane, 1960s, made in Japan, 4-3/4" h, **$30+.**

Holiday harps, 1970s, made in Japan, 4" h, **$25+.**

Holiday eggheads, 1980s, made in Western Germany, 4-5/8" and 4-1/4" h, **$30+.**

Roly-poly Santa and Mrs. Claus, 1960s, made in Japan, 3-1/2" h, **$35+.**

Roly-poly Santas, age unknown, unmarked, 3-1/2" h, **$25+.**

Santa serenade on the moon, 1970s, unmarked, 3-1/8" h, **$20+.**

Santa and Mrs. Claus in rocking chairs, 1970s, made in Japan, 3-3/4" h, **$35+.**

Santa and Mrs. Claus with sack and mitten, 1970s, unmarked, 3-3/4" and 3-1/2" h, **$25+.**

Santa and Mrs. Claus with sacks, 1960s, made in Japan, 4" and 3/4" h, **$25+.**

Santa and Mrs. Claus in sleigh, late 1960s, made in Japan, 5" long, **$35-$45.**

Santa and Mrs. Claus in sleighs, 1960s, made in Japan by Lefton, 3-3/4" h, **$35+.**

Santa and Mrs. Claus in teacups, contemporary, made by Lenox, 3-1/2" h, **$35-$45.**

Santa and Mrs. Claus with wreaths, 1980s, unmarked, 5" h and 4-3/4" h, **$25+.**

Snowman and woman heads, 1960s, unmarked, 3" h, **$25+.**

Snowmen in wooden sleigh, contemporary, snowmen 4" h, sleigh 6-3/4" long, **$25+.**

Victorian holiday shoppers, contemporary, made in China, 5-1/2" and 6" h, **$25+.**

White reindeer, 1960s, made in Japan, 3-1/2" h, **$30+.**

CLOWN SHAKERS

Comedic clowns are some of the most popular performers at circuses, parades and other events, and these shakers perfectly capture just some of their entertaining antics.

Acrobat clowns, 1960s, made in Japan, 2-1/2" h, **$20+.**

Clown with dog, 1940s, made in Japan, 4" and 2-3/4" h, **$40+.**

Clown on a drum, 1960s, made in Japan, 4-1/4" h overall, **$20+.**

Clown serenade, 1960s, made in Japan, 3-1/2" and 3-3/8" h, **$20+.**

Clown heads, 1950s, made in Japan, 4-1/4" h, **$25+.**

Clown heads on drums, 1950s, made in Japan, 3-3/4" h, **$25+.**

Clowns on donkeys, 1950s, made in Japan, 3" h, **$20+.**

Clowns in blue hats, 1950s, made in Japan, 3-1/2" h, **$20+.**

Clowns in green hats, 1950s, made in Japan, 3-1/2" h, **$20+.**

Clowns with gold trim, 1960s, made in Japan by Lefton, 4" and 3-3/4" h, **$25+.**

Lady clowns in handled tray, 1940s, made in Japan, 3″ h overall, **$40+.**

Luster-ware waving clowns, 1950s, made in Japan, 3-1/4″ h, **$25+.**

Mr. and Mrs. Clown, contemporary, unmarked, 3″ h, **$20+.**

Trumpeting clowns, 1960s, made in Japan, 3-1/2" h, **$20+.**

Tumbling clowns, 1950s, made in Japan, 3" and 2-3/4" h, **$20+.**

Waving clowns, 1950s, made in Japan, 3" h, **$25+.**

ETHNIC SHAKERS

The shakers pictured here include stereotyped images of cultures and races. When produced, some were thought of as humorous depictions, but today these are more often seen as offensive and condescending. For good or ill, they are a part of our cultural legacy and remain a popular collecting category.

African children, 1988, made in Korea, 2-3/4" and 2-1/2" h, **$25+.**

Kissing African couple on wooden bench, 1960s, marked Japan, 4" h and wide, **$30-$40.**

Black boys in caps, 1950s, marked Japan, 3-1/4" h, **$30-$40.**

Black mammy and butler, contemporary, 3″ and 3-3/8″ h, **$10-$15.**

Black mammy and butler, plastic, 1950s, marked F&F Mold and Die Works – Made in USA, 3-1/2″ h, **$55+.**

Black butler and mammy, plastic, 1950s, marked F&F Mold and Die Works – Made in USA, 5″ h, **$70+.**

Black mammy and chef, 1940s, 4-1/2″ h, **$30-$40.**

Black mammy and chef, contemporary, souvenir of New Orleans, 4-1/4" h, **$25+.**

Black chef and mammy with duck, contemporary, unmarked, 5" h, **$25-$35.**

Black mammy and chef with golf trim, 1940s, unmarked, 5-1/8" and 5-1/4" h, **$65+.**

Black chefs, contemporary, unmarked, 4" h, **$15-$20.**

Black figure, nodder, with watermelon wedge, 1950s, marked Japan, 3-1/2" h, **$250+.** (See Nodding Shakers, P. 142.)

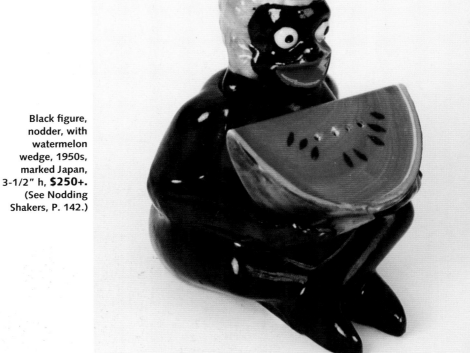

Black man wearing beret and watermelon wedge, 1950s, marked Japan, 2-1/2" h and 3" long, **$55-$65.**

Brown-skin chefs, 1950s, marked Japan, 3" h, **$25+.**

Alpine kids, 1940s, made in Czechoslovakia, 2-3/4" h, **$35-$45.**

Arab children, 1940s, marked Japan, 4-1/4" h, **$45.**

Englishmen in hats, 1950s, made in England, 2-1/2" h, **$20+.**

Ethnic heads, 1950s, made in Japan, 2-1/2" and 2-3/4" h, **$20+.**

Indian heads,
1950s, made in
Japan, 2-3/4" h,
$30+.

Indians, 1950s, marked
Niagara Falls, Canada,
2-1/2" h, **$25+.**

Indians in feathers
and war paint,
1950s, marked
Japan, 4" h, **$45+.**

Geisha and peasant, 1950s, made in Japan,
3-3/4" h, **$20+.**

Little Indians, 1960s,
made in Japan, 4-1/4" h,
$25-$35.

Oriental water carrier, 1940s, Occupied Japan,
4" h, **$25-$35.**

Oriental children, 1950s, marked Germany,
2-3/4" h, **$65-$75.**

MINIATURE SHAKERS

Some might argue that shakers made in the form of other objects are miniature to begin with. Most of the shakers in this section are tiny novelties and represent a popular collecting category.

Balsamic vinegar and olive oil bottles, contemporary, 1-3/4" and 2" h, **$20-$30.**

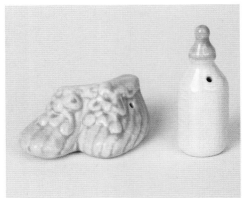

Baby booties and bottle, 1950s, 2" h and long, **$20-$30.**

Birthday cards, contemporary, 1-5/8" h, **$20-$30.**

Cake and slice, 1-1/2" and 2" diameter without utensils, **$35-$40.**

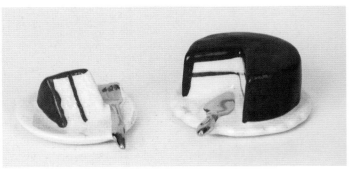

Candleholders, 1-3/8" h, **$20-$30.**

Cowboy boots with spurs, 2" h, **$20-$30.**

Coal scuttle and potbellied stove, 1-1/4" and 2-3/8" h, **$20-$30.**

Sleeping dog with bone, 1-3/4" and 2" long, **$20-$30.**

Ethnic children,
1-3/4" h,
$20-$30.

Dustpan and broom,
each 1-1/2" long,
$20-$30.

Gingerbread boy
and rolling pin,
each 2" long,
$20-$30.

Guitar and accor-
dion, 2-1/2" long
and 1-1/2" h,
$35-$40.

Butter churn and
milk can, 2" and
1/2" h, **$35-$40.**

Pocket watch and coin purse, each 1-1/8" long, **$35-$40.**

Suitcase and valise, 1-1/2" and 1-1/4" long, **$35-$40.**

Thimble and spool, 1" and 1-1/8" h, **$20-$30.**

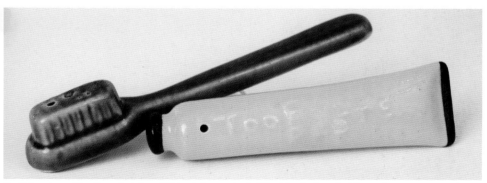

Toothbrush and toothpaste tube, 1930s, tube marked, "Toof Paste," probably made in Japan, 4-3/4" and 3-3/4" long, **$25-$35.**

MUFFINEERS

Salt and pepper shakers evolved from the English "muffineer" or sugar shaker.

Cranberry glass in a reeded pattern, contemporary, 4-1/4" h, **$50-$65.**

Lead crystal, Primrose pattern (?), maker and age unknown, possibly German, 4-3/4" h, **$45.**

Milk-glass in a grape motif, maker unknown, 1990s, 4-1/2" h, **$75-$100.**

Moon-and-Stars pattern, maker unknown, 1950s-60s, 4-1/2" h, **$65-$75.**

Three Face pattern, frosted and clear glass, footed, from a Duncan & Miller mold, early 1900s, 5" h, **$250.**

NODDING SHAKERS

Before there were bobble-heads, there were "nodders." In this case, little figural shakers that sit in a holder and pivot in a nodding motion. As you might expect, they are fragile and easily damaged, so they often have a premium price.

Bass, late 1940s, made in Japan, 3" h overall, **$65-$75.**

Mr. and Mrs. Cat, contemporary, marked "Clay Art – Made in China," car 5" long, **$25-$35.**

Ribbon cats, 1940s, souvenir of Chillicothe, Ohio, made in Japan, 3-3/4" h, **$65-$75.**

Ducks, late 1940s, made in Japan, 3-1/4" h overall, **$65-$75.**

Fawns, 1950s, made in Japan, 4" h, **$55-$65.**

Game birds, 1950s, made in Japan, 3-1/2" h, **$55-$65.**

Hen and rooster with condiment holder, 1940s, Occupied Japan, 5" wide, **$125-$150.**

Hen and rooster, 1950s, souvenir of Grand Coulee Dam, made in Japan, 3-1/2" h, **$55-$65.**

Indians in decorated base, souvenir of Walla Walla, Wash., 1950s, made in Japan, 3-1/4" h, **$65-$75.**

Indians in a drum, 1950s, made in Japan, 3-1/2" h, **$65-$75.**

Kangaroo and joey, 1950s, made in Japan, 4-1/4" h, **$65.**

Pheasants, 1950s, made in Japan, 3-1/8" h, **$55-$65.**

Pretentious pigs, late 1940s, made in Japan, 4" h, **$200-$225.**

Pretentious pigs, with gold trim, late 1940s, made in Japan, 4" h, **$200-$225.**

Skulls with rhinestone eyes, souvenir of Louisville, Ky., 1950s, made in Japan, 3-1/2" h overall, **$55-$65.**

Snake charmer and cobra, 1950s, made in Japan, 3-1/4" and 4" h, **$125-$150.**

Turkeys, late 1940s, made in Japan, 3-1/4" h overall, **$65-$75.**

Shakers By Maker

Nearly 40 manufacturers are represented in this section. Remember that many glass companies bought and sold molds, so one firm's early designs may show up in other colors when reused by another maker. For more information, contact the National Novelty Salt and Pepper Shakers Collectors Club at www.saltandpepperclub.com, or the Antique and Art Glass Salt Shaker Collector's Society Inc. at www.antiquesaltshakers.com. Collectors Jim Langer and Doug Horton, the main contributors to this guide, may also be reached at 612-623-0134.

Manufacturers in this chapter are listed alphabetically, and shakers are also listed alphabetically within in their respective sections.

AMERICAN BISQUE

The American Bisque Pottery Co. of Williamstown, W.V., was founded in 1919 to produce china doll heads, which had become difficult to import from Germany during World War I. Production expanded to include cookie jars, bowls, serving dishes, ashtrays and kitchenwares. The company closed in 1983.

Bears, which coordinate with cookie jars, 1950s, 3-1/4" h, **$45-$50.**

Bouquet bears, without color, 1940s, 4-3/8" h, **$55-$65.**

Bouquet bears, with cold-painted color and larger ears, 1940s, 4-3/8" h, **$65-$75.**

Bears with cookies, 1950s, 3-1/4" h, **$55-$65.**

Bears with cookies, and gold trim, 1950s, 3-1/4" h, **$75-$85.**

Teddy bears, with gold trim, 1950s, 3-1/4" h, **$75-$85.**

Teddy bears, 1950s, 3-1/4" h, **$45-$55.**

Chicks, with gold trim, 1950s, 3-1/4" h, **$75-$85.**

Cows, 1950s, souvenir of Chicago, 3-1/4" h, **$45-$55.**

Ducklings, 1950s, 3-1/4" h, **$55-$65.**

Baby elephants, 1950s, 3-1/2" h, **$45-$55.**

Baby elephants, 1950s, 3-1/2" h, **$45-$55.**

Lambs, red trim, different from cookie jars, 1950s, 3-1/4" h, **$45-$55.**

Lambs, blue trim, different from cookie jars, 1950s, 3-1/4" h, **$45-$55.**

Dating or tilt-head lambs, with cold-paint decoration, 1940s, 4-1/2" h, **$65-$75.**

Lambs, kitchen size, cold paint, 1940s, marked USA, 4-3/4" h, **$95-$105.**

Bowtie pigs, 1950s, 3-1/4" h, **$55-$65.**

Dancing Pig, which coordinates with cookie jar, 1950s, 4-1/8" h, **$80-$90.**

Dancing Pig, which coordinates with cookie jar, 1950s, 4-1/8" h, **$80-$90.**

Mr. and Mrs. Pig, 1950s, 3-1/2" h, **$45-$50.**

Mr. and Mrs. Pig, with gold trim, 1950s, 3-1/2" h, **$65-$75.**

Proud pigs, 1950s, 3-1/4" h, **$45-$50**; similar to Shawnee's Smiley Pig.

Proud pigs, 1950s, 3-1/4" h, **$45-$50**.

Chubby chefs, kitchen size, 1960s, 5" h, unmarked, **$45-$55**.

Clowns, which coordinate with cookie jars, 1950s, 3-1/2" h, **$65-$75**.

Donald Duck, with gold trim, late 1940s, sometimes marked Disney, this pair also marked "Harding Memorial and Museum, Marion, Ohio," 3-1/4" h, **$100+**.

Donald Duck with red fez, similar to cookie jar but head is turned, 1940s, 3-1/2" h, **$85-$95**.

Donald Duck with blue fez, similar to cookie jar but head is turned, 1940s, 3-1/2" h, **$85-$95.**

Dumbo, without color, 1950s, sometimes marked Disney, 3-1/2" h, **$55-$65.**

Dumbo, with color, 1950s, sometimes marked Disney, 3-1/2" h, **$75-$85.**

Mickey and Minnie Mouse, 1950s, sometimes marked Disney, 3-1/4″ h, **$75-$100.**

Pluto, 1950s, marked Disney, 3-1/4″ h, **$85-$95.**

Thumper, late 1940s, marked Disney, 3-1/4″ h, **$75-$85.**

HOCKING GLASS CO./ANCHOR HOCKING GLASS CORP.

Hocking Glass Co. was established in 1905, and named for the river that runs through Lancaster, Ohio. Its first factory was known as the Black Cat because of the haze of carbon dust that hung in the air. In 1937, the Anchor Cap and Closure Corp. merged with Hocking Glass to become Anchor Hocking Glass Corp. The word "Glass" was dropped from the company's name in 1969. The firm's headquarters are still in Lancaster.

Anchor Hocking Glass Corp., Manhattan pattern, late 1930s to early '40s, 2-5/8" h, **$30+.**

Anchor Hocking Glass Corp., Queen Mary pattern, late 1930s to early '40s, 2-5/8" h, **$30+.**

Anchor Hocking Glass Corp., Royal Ruby, 1940s-60s, 3-3/4" h, no established value.

Hocking Glass Co., yellow Block Optic pattern, footed, circa 1930, 4-1/4" h, **$115+.**

Hocking Glass Co., green Cameo pattern, footed, also called Dancing Girl or Ballerina, early to mid-1930s, 4" h, **$85-$100.**

Hocking Glass Co., green Dove (?) pattern, mid-1930s, 6" h, **$85+.**

Hocking Glass Co., Lake Como pattern, with transfer decoration, 1930s, 3-1/4" h, **$50+.**

Hocking Glass Co., pink Miss America pattern, footed, mid-1930s, note difference in tapered and swelling profile above foot, 4-1/4" h, **$75-$85.**

Hocking Glass Co., green
Princess pattern, early 1930s,
4-1/2" h, **$75+.**

Hocking Glass Co., green Squat Block Optic pattern, circa 1930, 3" h, **$135+.**

BELLAIR GOBLET CO.

The Bellaire Goblet Co. was established in Bellaire, Ohio, in 1876 and moved to Findlay, Ohio, in 1888. The company joined the U. S. Glass Co. combine in 1891 as Factory M. It closed in 1892.

Log and Star pattern, crystal, late 1800s, 3-1/2" h, **$45-$55.**

CAMBRIDGE GLASS CO.

The Cambridge (Ohio) Glass Co. began production in 1902. The firm initially used the molds of other companies to make table sets, jugs, bowls, jars, tumblers and lamps. In the 1930s, about 700 people were employed. The company closed in 1954, and after several attempts to reopen, Imperial Glass Co. of Bellaire, Ohio, bought the Cambridge molds in 1960.

Amber glass with crystal handled tray, 1930s; shakers 2-3/4" h, tray 5-1/4" h, $75+ set.

Ball form in amethyst glass, with Farber Bros. metal bases, 1940s, $45-$55.

Caprice pattern, footed, Alpine finish, 1940s-50s, 1-3/4" h, $75.

Caprice pattern, footed, crystal, 1940s-50s, 1-3/4" h, **$60.**

Caprice pattern, Moonlight Blue, 1940s-50s, 3" h, **$75-$85.**

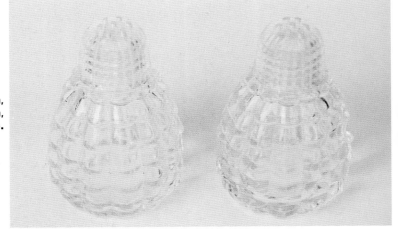

Cascade pattern, 1950s, 3" h, **$20+.**

Chantilly pattern, 1940s-50s, 3 h, **$45+.**

Chantilly pattern, 1940s-50s, 3-3/4" h, **$50+.**

Decagon pattern, footed, black glass, found in three sizes, 1930s, 4-1/4" h, **$65.**

Decagon pattern, footed, in Bluebell, 1926-30s, 4-1/4" h, **$95.**

Ebony with crystal handled tray, 1920s; shakers 3″ h, tray 5-1/2″ h, **$75+** set.

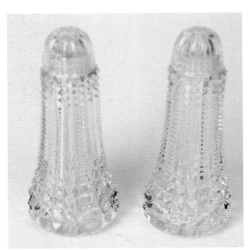

Martha pattern, 1940s-50s, 4-3/4″ h, **$45+**.

Mount Vernon pattern, 1920s-40s, 3-1/2″ h, **$35+**.

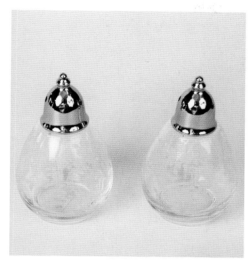

Rose Point pattern, 1930s-50s, 2-3/4" h, **$45+.**

Rose Point pattern, 1930s-50s, 3-1/2" h, **$55+.**

Square pattern, 1949-50s, 3-1/2" h, **$25+.**

Wildflower Etched pattern, footed, 1940s-50s, 4" h, **$55-$65.**

CERAMIC ARTS STUDIO

Ceramic Arts Studio of Madison, Wis., produced decorative figurines, wall plaques, shakers and head vases from 1942 until the business closed in 1956. Artist Betty Harrington designed more than 800 figurines for the company.

Asian children, 4-1/2" h, **$65-$75.**

Dutch children, 4" h, **$65-$75.**

"Wee People" Dutch children, 3" h, **$65-$75.**

"Wee People" French children, 3-1/4" h, **$80-$90.**

"Wee People" German children, 3-1/3" and 3" h, **$80-$90.**

"Wee People" Indian children, 3-1/4" and 3" h, **$50-$60.**

"Wee People" Oriental children, 3" h, also with souvenir decal from Oregon, **$65-$75.**

"Wee People" Scottish children, 3-1/2" and 3" h, **$70-$80.**

Brown bear and cub "snugglers," 4-1/2" and 2-1/4" h, **$65-$75.**

Polar bear and cub "snugglers," 4-1/2" and 2-1/4" h, **$65-$75.**

Siamese mother cat and kitten, 4-1/4" and 3" h, **$65-$75.**

Nestling Siamese cats, known as Thai and Thai-Thai, 4-1/4" and 5" long, **$75-$85.**

Fighting cocks, 3-1/2"
and 4" h, **$75-$85.**

Chimp mother and baby, 4" and 2-1/2" h,
$65-$75.

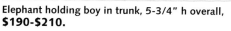

Elephant holding boy in trunk, 5-3/4" h overall,
$190-$210.

Elephant couple, 3-3/4" and 3-1/4" h, **$60-$70.**

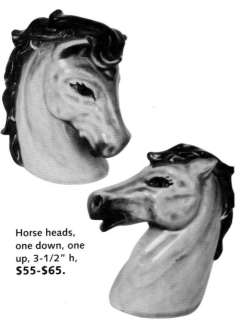

Horse heads, one down, one up, 3-1/2" h, **$55-$65.**

Kangaroo mother and joey, 4-3/4" and 2-1/4" h, **$150-$175.**

Mouse and cheese, mouse 2" h, cheese 3" long, **$35-$45.**

Skunk mother and child, 3-3/4" and 2" h, **$50-$60.**

Tropical fish with atypical glaze, 3-3/4" h, **$150-$175.**

Tropical fish with traditional glaze and modeling, 4-1/4" h, **$100-$125.**

CHALLINOR, TAYLOR & CO.

Challinor, Taylor & Co. Ltd. was organized in 1885 in Tarentum, Pa. It specialized in tableware, novelties, opaque and mosaic (marble or slag) glass. The company joined the U.S. Glass combine in 1891.

Challinor, Taylor & Co. shakers in Milk-glass, Forget-Me-Not pattern, 1889-1891, 2-3/4" h without caps, **$65-$75.**

CONSOLIDATED LAMP & GLASS CO.

The Consolidated Lamp & Glass Co. of Coraopolis, Pa., was founded in 1894. The company made lamps, tableware and art glass. In 1928, the firm introduced the "Ruba Rombic" line of Art Deco glassware. The factory was destroyed by fire in 1963.

Bulging Petal pattern, marbleized pastel, late 1800s, 2-1/2" h, $80-$100.

Bulging Three Petal pattern, late 1800s, 2-1/4" h, $65-$75.

Cord and Tassel pattern, marbleized pastel, late 1800s, 2" h, $125-$150.

Cotton Bale pattern, sold in mixed pastel colors and found in other combinations, late 1800s, 2-3/4" h, **$75-$100.**

Florette pattern, late 1800s, 2-1/2" h, **$150-$175.**

Guttate pattern, ruby overlay, later version of an old Consolidated mold, 3-1/4" h, **$75-$100.**

Leaf Layers pattern, late 1800s, 2-1/2" diameter, **$125-$150.**

Overlapping Shell pattern, late 1800s, 3" h, **$150-$175.**

Pineapple pattern, late 1800s, 3-1/2" h, **$85-$100.**

Periwinkle pattern, late 1800s, 2-5/8" h with cap, showing "bust-off" jagged top at right, **$125-$150.**

DITHRIDGE & CO.

Edward Dithridge was born in Birmingham, England, on Aug. 22, 1804, and immigrated to the United States in 1812. Dithridge & Co.'s Fort Pitt Glass Works of Pittsburgh was established in 1827, making lamps and lamp chimneys, reflectors, bouquet holders, curtain pins, mortars and pestles, goblets, spoon holders, salts, celeries, candlesticks, bowls, cake stands, cigar and match holders, card receivers and paperweights. The firm merged with the Pittsburgh Lamp, Brass & Glass Co. in 1903.

Beaded Bottom pattern, sold in mixed colors and found in other combinations, 1898-1900, 3-3/8" h, \$125+.

Creased Bale pattern, late 1800s, found in other colors, 3" h, \$70-\$80.

Double Fan Band pattern, made in other opaque colors, late 1800s, 3-3/4" h, \$65-\$75.

Double Leaf, made in other opaque colors, late 1800s, 3-3/4" h, **$175-$200.**

Square Scroll pattern, made in other opaque colors, late 1800s, 3-1/2" h, **$75-$100.**

Little Shrimp pattern, circa 1900, 2-1/4" diameter, **$85.**

Spider Web pattern, in Milk-glass, found in other pastel colors, 1894-1897, unmarked, 2-3/4" h, **$65.**

DUNCAN & MILLER

The Geo. Duncan & Sons glass factory was founded in 1874 in Pittsburgh, Pa. In 1893, sons James and Harry Duncan and John E. Miller, who had been a supervisor of the Pittsburgh factory mold shop, opened their own factory in Washington, Pa. After James died in 1900, Miller became a full partner and the factory became Duncan & Miller. The company closed in 1955; most of the molds and equipment were acquired by the U.S. Glass Co.

No. 308 Block pattern, crystal, circa 1900, 2-3/4" h, **$45-$55.**

Canterbury pattern, crystal, 1940s, 4" h, **$45-$55.**

Mardi Gras pattern, crystal, early 1900s, unmarked, 3-1/4" h, **$75.**

EAGLE GLASS AND MANUFACTURING CO.

Eagle Glass and Manufacturing Co. of Wellsburg, W.V., was founded in 1894 as a decorative-glass factory. The firm also made metal lids for glass jars and supplied cans for the railroad industry.

Bow & Tassel pattern, circa 1900, showing color variation common to early Milk-glass, 3-3/4" h, **$40-$50.**

Four-Footed Scroll, late 1800s, 4" h, **$45-$60.**

Grape pattern, early 1900s, 2-1/2" and 3" h, would have come with a tray, unmarked, **$75;** with tray, **$100.**

Open Flower pattern, early 1900s, 3-1/2" h, **$40-$50.**

FEDERAL GLASS CO.

The Federal Glass Co. of Columbus, Ohio, was founded in 1900. The firm made salt and pepper shakers, goblets, measuring cups and jars. Federal closed in 1980.

Patrician, sometimes called Spoke, mid-1930s, also found in amber and green, 4" h, **$125.**

Normandy, 1930s, showing color variation, 4" h, **$50.**

Sharon, sometimes called Cabbage Rose, 1930s, 2-3/4" h, **$75+.**

FENTON ART GLASS CO.

The Fenton Art Glass Co. was founded in 1905 by Frank L. Fenton and his brother, John W., in an old glass factory in Martins Ferry, Ohio. They initially sold hand-painted glass made by other manufacturers, but it wasn't long before they decided to produce their own glass. The new Fenton factory in Williamstown, W.V., opened on Jan. 2, 1907.

Three generations later, the firm's president and CEO, George M. Fenton, announced on Aug. 9, 2007, that the 102-year-old company would immediately lay off 25 of its 150 employees and cease taking orders at the end of the month. However, a late surge of orders allowed the company to remain open into 2008.

Most Fenton shakers listed here are priced individually, and arranged by year of production.

Crystal and Jade Green in Diamond Optic (the pattern is on the inside of the Jade Green shaker), late 1920s, 4-1/2" h; Crystal, $30-$40; Jade Green, $50-$75.

Turquoise, "Skim" Milk-glass, French Opalescent and Blue Opalescent in "5 & 6" Hobnail, 1940s, 3-1/2" h; Milk-glass, $15; others, $30+ each.

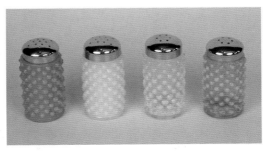

Black (Ebony), Milk-glass and Ruby Overlay in a swirl pattern, 1950s, 2-1/2" h; Black (Ebony), **$25**; Milk-glass, **$15+**; Ruby Overlay, **$50+**.

Blue Opalescent, French Opalescent and Topaz Opalescent in footed Hobnail, 1940s, 3-1/2" h; Blue and French, **$40+** each; Topaz, **$60+**.

Blue Overlay in Floral Sprig, made for L.G. Wright, 1940s, 3-1/2" h, **$75+** pair.

Sugar shaker or muffineer, Cranberry Polka Dot overlay, 1940s, 4-3/4" h, **$195+**.

Sugar shaker or muffineer, large Bubble Optic in Cranberry, 1940s, 4-3/4" h, **$225+.**

Sugar shaker or muffineer, Topaz Opalescent in Daisy and Fern, 1940s, 4-1/2" h, **$250+.**

Rainbow bulbous pair of salt and pepper shakers, opal cased, satin finish, original two-part lids, undamaged, wear to tops, probably European, early 20th century, 3 3/4" h overall, **$3,390** pair. Property of the Fenton Art Glass Museum. *Photo courtesy Green Valley Auctions Inc., Mt. Crawford, Va.*

Cranberry Opalescent and Topaz Opalescent (1940s) and Plum Opalescent (1990s) in "5 & 5" Hobnail, 3-1/2" h; Cranberry, **$60+**, Topaz and Plum, **$75+** each.

Two pairs of New World in Cranberry Opalescent and Green Opalescent Rib Optic, 1950s, sold in pairs of two sizes, 4" h and 5" h; Cranberry, **$175** pair; Green, rare, **$300** pair.

Rose Pastel and Green Pastel in Lamb's Tongue, 1954-55, 3-1/2" h, **$40+** each.

Milk-glass, Green Pastel and Rose Pastel in a swirl pattern, mid-1950s, 3-1/2" h; Milk-glass, **$15+**; pastels, **$25+** each.

Milk-glass, French Opalescent and Black (Ebony) in "5 & 5" Hobnail, 1940s, 3-1/2" h; Milk-glass, **$15**; French and Black, **$30** each.

Amber and Ruby footed in Georgian (found in eight colors), 1931-39; Ruby, **$65+**; Amber, **$35+**.

Two styles of Silver Crest, 4-1/2" and 5" h, **$125+** each pair.

Ruby in Diamond Optic, pewter tops, 1930s, 4-1/2" h, **$200+** pair.

Silver Crest "bowling pins," 1940s, very rare, each 4" h, **$400+** pair.

Blue Pastel, Milk-glass and black (Ebony) in Block and Star, mid-1950s, 3-1/2" h, **$40+** each.

Colonial Amber and Colonial Green in Valencia, 1960s-70s, 5" h, **$35+** each.

Colonial Amber, Blue and Green footed in Thumb Print, and a Black (Ebony) example sold only through Fenton gift shop, 1960s-70s, 3-1/2" h; Colonial Blue, **$50+**; Amber and Green, **$25+** each; Black (Ebony), no established value.

Colonial Amber, Colonial Pink and Colonial Blue in Thumb Print (flat bottom), 1960s to 1970s, 4" h; Pink and Blue, **$35+** each; Amber, **$15+**.

Colonial Blue, Milk-glass, Colonial Amber, Colonial Green and Colonial Orange in Daisy and Button, 1970s, 3-1/2" h; Blue, **$20+**; Milk-glass, **$10+**; Amber, Green and Orange, **$15+** each.

Colonial Blue, Amber, Milk-glass (1960s-70s) and Blue Iridized (QVC, 1990s) in Rose pattern, 3-1/2" to 4-1/2" h; Colonial Blue, **$30+**; Amber and Milk-glass, **$20** each, and Blue Iridized, **$25+**.

Cranberry Polka Dot (1955) and Yellow Legacy Rib Optic (1970s), 2-1/2" h; Cranberry, **$65+**; Yellow (Candle Glow), **$23+**.

Crystal (1970s) and Original Formula Carnival Glass (1990s) in Fine Cut and Block, and Milk-glass in Old Virginia (1960s), 4" h; crystal and Milk-glass, **$15+** each; OFCG, **$35+**.

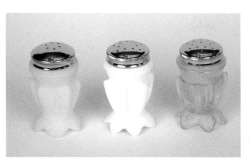

Custard, Milk-glass and Topaz Opalescent in Cactus, early 1960s to 1970s, 3-1/2" h; Custard, **$25+**; Milk, **$15+**; Topaz, **$45+**.

Condiment set in Flower Panel, sold in Milk-glass and Jamestown Blue as shown, 1957-58, **$150+** set; single Milk-glass shaker, **$25+**.

Honey Amber Overlay and Milk-glass in Wild Rose and Bowknot, 1960s, 3-1/2" h to 4-1/2" h; Honey Amber, **$35+**; Milk-glass, **$15+**.

Honey Amber Overlay, Milk-glass, Powder Blue Overlay and Apple Green Overlay in Jacqueline, 1960s, 2-1/2" h; Milk-glass, **$20+**; Honey, Blue and Green, **$35+**.

Midnight Blue, Amber and Blue Opalescent in Hobnail, 1970s, 3-1/2" h, **$30+** each.

Milk-glass condiment set (salt, pepper, mustard and stand) in Tear Drop, late 1950s, 7" h with handle, **$95+** set.

Milk-glass and Topaz Opalescent, 1970s, 4-1/2" h, Milk-glass, **$25+**; Topaz (marked), **$45+**.

Ruby, Milk-glass and Colonial Green in Thumb Print (flat bottom), 1960s to 1970s, 4" h; Ruby, **$50+**; Milk and Green, **$15+**.

Ruby Overlay in Dot Optic and Jamestown shaker in Polka Dot, 1955, 2-1/2" h, **$45+** each.

Yellow in Rib Optic, made for Foreman, 1970s, 4" h (would have been paired with a taller example), **$45+** each.

Blue, Green and Black (Ebony) in a swirl pattern, hand painted, 1990s, 2-1/2" h, **$25+** each.

Three hand-painted in Tear Drop, 1990s, 2-1/2" h, **$20+** each.

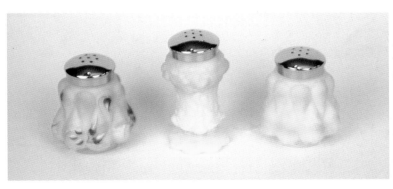

Three Burmese, two in Tear Drop (one hand painted), one in Rose, 1990s, 2-1/2" h and 3-1/2" h; Rose and plain Tear Drop, **$50+** each; hand-painted Tear Drop, **$75+**.

Champagne Satin, Ruby and Amber Iridized in Daisy and Button, late 1990s to 2000, 3-1/2" h, **$20+** each.

New World in Cobalt
Opalescent Rib
Optic, 2000, made
for QVC, 5″ h,
$125+ pair.

Green, Iridized
Opalescent and
Purple in Daisy
and Button, late
1990s to 2000,
3-1/2″ h,
$20+ each.

From left: Crystal in Regency, Light Blue and Crystal in Flower Band, and Crystal in Strawberry, 1980s, each approximately 3-1/2″ h, **$15-$20** each.

Two pairs of New World in Plum Opalescent and Topaz Opalescent in Rib Optic, made for the National Fenton Glass Society, early 2000s, 4″ h and 5″ h; Plum, **$125+** pair; Topaz, **$150+** pair.

Ruby Overlay in Leaf, 1990s, 3-1/2″ h, **$50+.**

FOSTORIA GLASS CO.

The Fostoria (Ohio) Glass Co. began operations in 1887. The firm's American pattern, introduced in 1915, is still being produced by Lancaster Colony, which bought Fostoria in 1983, and closed the plant in 1986.

American pattern, 3" h, **$45-$55.**

American pattern, individual with tray, 2-1/2" h, tray 4" long, **$45-$55.**

Baroque pattern with Chintz etching, 1940-70s, 2-3/4" h, **$100-$125.**

Cape Cod pattern, limited edition made for Avon, 1978, 4-1/2" h, **$25+.**

Centennial pattern, footed, 1980s, 4-3/4" h, **$25+.**

Century pattern, 1950s-80s, 3" h, **$35+.**

Century, with tray, 1950s-80s, 2-1/2" h, tray 4-1/4" long, **$45+** set.

Coin pattern, 1950s-70s, made in six colors, 3-1/4" h, **$100-$125** in blue.

Coin pattern, 1950s-70s, made in six colors, 3-1/4" h, **$100-$125** in ruby.

Colony, 1930s-70s, 3-1/4" h, **$25+.**

Colony, 1930s-70s, 4" h, **$35+.**

Fairfax, footed, 1920s-40s, 3-1/4" h, **$75-$100.**

Fairfax, footed ebony, 1920s-40s, 3-1/4" h, **$100-$125.**

Individual shakers in three colors, 1930s, found in other colors and crystal, 2-1/4" h, **$25** each pair.

Jamestown pattern, late 1950s-80s, found in eight colors, 3-1/2" h, **$50-$65.**

Knobby pattern, early 1900s, 3-1/2" h, **$65-$75.**

Monaco pattern, 1970s-80s, 2-3/4" h, **$25-$35.**

Mayfair pattern, 1920s-30s, 3-3/4" h, **$75+.**

Pebble Beach pattern, 1960s-70s, 3″ h, **$50-$65.**

Sonata pattern, footed, 1960s, 3″ h, **$25-$35.**

Sunray pattern, 1950s-60s, 4″ h, **$40-$50.**

FRANCISCAN POTTERY

Gladding, McBean & Co. began making Franciscan dinnerware in 1934 at a plant in Glendale, Calif. Apple (1940) and Desert Rose (1941) are the only continuously produced Franciscan patterns, and remain in production today. The American Franciscan factory closed in 1984.

Apple, introduced 1940, hand painted, 2-1/2" h, **$25+.**

Desert Rose, introduced 1941, hand painted, 2-3/4" h, **$25+.**

GILLANDER GLASS CO.

Gillinder Glass Co. was founded in 1861 by English immigrant William T. Gillinder (1823-1871). The Philadelphia firm manufactured primarily glass chimneys and other components for lamps, but it also produced molded and cut glass, silvered tablewares, doorknobs and other household items. When Gillinder's two sons, James and Frederick, joined the company in 1867, the name was changed to Gillinder and Sons.

Now based in Port Jervis, N.Y., Gillinder Glass makes products for industrial and commercial lighting, and reproduction lighting devices for historic preservation projects.

Gillinder & Sons, Scrolled Rib pattern, late 1800s, sold in mixed colors, 3" h, **$60-$75.**

GOEBEL

W. Goebel Porzellanfabrik, founded in 1871, is a manufacturer of figurines and tableware, most notably the childhood designs of Sister Maria Innocentia Hummel, who died of tuberculosis in 1946 at the age of 37.

Black children, 1930s, made in Germany, possibly Goebel, 3" h, **$60-$70.**

East Indian children, 1950s, marked Germany, 3-1/4" h, **$35+.**

German children huggers, 1950s, marked Bad Nauheim, also marked with bee and V, 3-1/4" h, **$65-$75.**

Hooded children holding tankard, carrot, heart and flower, 1960s, 2-3/4" h, **$65-$75.**

Victorian children, 1940s, marked with bee and V, 2-3/4" h, **$75-$85.**

Victorian children, 1950s, marked Germany, 3" h, **$85-$95.**

Ducks, 1960s, marked with bee and V, 2-3/4" long, **$45-$55.**

Pheasants, 1950s, marked with bee and V, 3-3/4" and 4-1/2" long, **$35-$45.**

Black and white poodles, 1950s, 3-1/2" and 3" h, **$40+.**

Tropical fish, 1960s, marked W. Germany, 2-3/4" h, **$45-$55.**

Winking chef and cook, 1940s, 3-3/4" h, **$55-$65.**

Cowboy and cowgirl huggers, 1950s, 3" h, **$45-$55.**

Santas, 1960s, marked Western Germany, 2-3/4" h, **$65-$75.**

Monks,
1960s, marked
Western Germany,
2-1/2" h,
$45-$55.

Monks with books,
1960s, marked
with bee and V,
3-1/4" h,
$75-$85.

HAZEL-ATLAS GLASS CO.

The Hazel-Atlas Glass Co. was a large producer of machine-molded glass containers and headquartered in Wheeling, W.V. It was founded in 1902 in Washington, Pa., as the merger of four companies: Hazel Glass and Metals Co., Atlas Glass Co., Wheeling Metal Plant and Republic Glass Co. By the 1930s, Hazel-Atlas had 15 plants and was the largest glass manufacturer in the world. In 1956, Hazel-Atlas was acquired by the Continental Can Co.

Cloverleaf pattern, footed, early to mid-1930s, found in other colors, 3-3/4" h, **$50+.**

Florentine No. 1 pattern, footed, early 1930s, 4" h, **$45+.**

Florentine No. 2 pattern, footed, early 1930s, 4-1/4" h, **$45+.**

Hairpin pattern, footed, sometimes called Newport, 1940s, 4-3/8" h, **$25-$35.**

Moderntone, footed, mid-1930s-40s, 4-1/4" h, **$55+.**

New Century pattern, footed, early to mid-1930s, 4-1/4" h, **$50+.**

Royal Lace pattern, footed, 1930s, 4-1/4" h, **$75+.**

A. H. HEISEY & CO.

Augustus H. Heisey (1842-1922) was born in Hanover, Germany. His family immigrated to the United States in 1843 and settled in Pennsylvania. He became part owner of Geo. Duncan & Sons after his marriage to Susan Duncan, George's daughter. Heisey opened his own glass factory in Newark, Ohio, in 1896. The firm went out of business in 1957.

Bead Swag pattern in Opal glass, painted decoration, gold trim and transfer lettering, early 1900s, 3" h, $75-$100.

Cheshire pattern, Flamingo glass, found in other colors, 1925-35, 4-1/4" h, $85+.

Cross Line Flute pattern, 1920-30s, unmarked, 3" h, $125.

Crystolite pattern, 1930s-50s, 2-1/2" h, $40-$50.

Empress pattern, in Sahara Yellow glass, 1930-37, 3-1/4" h, **$125+.**

Fancy Loop pattern, crystal glass with gold trim, early 1900s, 3" h, **$100.**

Fancy Loop pattern, crystal glass, early 1900s, 3-3/8" h, **$100.**

Flat Panel pattern, individual, in Moon Gleam glass, found in other colors, 1925-35, 2-1/4" h, **$50.**

Kalonyal pattern, made only in crystal, 1906-09, 3-3/4" h, **$200+.**

Locket on Chain pattern, in Ruby flash with gold trim, 1898-1906, unmarked, 3" h, no established value.

Narrow Flute pattern, 1920s, marked in two places on each shaker with an H in a diamond, 2-3/4" h, **$40-$50.**

Narrow Flute with Rim pattern, with wheel-cut floral decoration, 1915-30s, 3" h, **$80-$90.**

Pineapple and Fan pattern, late 1800s to early 1900s, 2-3/4" h, **$100-$115.**

Plantation pattern, 1940s-50s, 3-1/4" h, **$100-$125.**

Prince of Wales pattern, individual, 1902-12, unmarked, 3" h, **$150.**

Provincial, made only in crystal, 1940s-50s, 3" h, **$35+.** This same pattern was made in other colors by Imperial.

Punty Band pattern in Ivorina Verde glass (custard), hand-painted souvenirs of Albany, Minn., early 1900s, 3" h, **$75-$85.**

Punty Band pattern, in Ruby flash, marked "Clara – Minnesota State Fair 1908," 3" h, **$75+.**

Spool pattern, individual, Flamingo glass, 1925-35, unmarked, 2-3/4" h, **$50-$60.**

Tall individual, in Moon Gleam glass, 3" h, **$75.**

Twist pattern, in Moon Gleam, found in other colors, 1925-35, 2-3/4" h, **$75+.**

Urn pattern, crystal glass, with #3 sanitary caps, circa 1910, unmarked, 3-5/8" h, **$125.** Heisey used four separate styles of sanitary caps: two with metal and glass, and two all glass.

Victorian pattern, with #1 sanitary cap, 1930s-50s, 3" h, **$85-$100.** Heisey used four separate styles of sanitary caps, two with metal and glass, and two all glass.

Waverly pattern, footed, with Orchid Etch, 1940s-50s, 4-1/4" h, **$75+.** The shakers in this pattern do not have an etched orchid, though other pieces do.

Waverly pattern, footed, with Rose Etch, 1940s-50s, 4-1/4" h, **$75+.**

Waverly pattern, footed, tri-corner base, silver anniversary motif, 1940s-50s, 4-1/4" h, **$55+.**

Waverly pattern, 1940s-50s, 3-1/2" h, **$55+.**

Wing Scroll pattern, in custard glass, circa 1900, unmarked, 3" h, **$200-$225.**

HOLT-HOWARD

The Holt-Howard Co. of Stamford, Conn., was founded in 1948 by A. Grant Holt and John and Robert Howard. They became famous as importers of whimsical ceramic items. The firm went out of business in 1990. Because Holt-Howard wares often had paper or foil labels, a collector must have a trained eye to spot unmarked examples.

Clumps of strawberries, 1960s, made in Japan, 3" h, **$15+.**

Mr. and Mrs. Snowman with presents, 1960s, made in Japan, 4" and 3-3/4" h, **$35+.**

Sixties rabbits with big eyes and flowers, made in Japan, 2-3/4" h, **$25+.**

IMPERIAL GLASS CO.

The Imperial Glass Co. was established in 1901 and moved to a plant in Bellaire, Ohio, in 1904. One of its most popular designs was Candlewick. Imperial acquired the assets of A.H. Heisey in 1958 and Cambridge Glass Works in 1960. Lenox bought the company in 1973, and Imperial ceased operations in 1983.

No. 612 pattern in vaseline, 1940s–50s, found in other colors, 4-1/4" h, $85-$100.

Candlewick, footed, 1936-48, 5-1/4" h, $75+.

Candlewick, 1936-48, 4" h, $25-$30.

Cape Cod pattern, with handled tray, 3" h and tray 3" wide, **$40-$50** set.

Cape Cod pattern, footed, introduced 1942, made for 40 years, 5-1/4" h, **$50-$65.**

Cape Cod pattern in Sunshine Yellow, found in other colors, 1970s, marked with conjoined "IG," 3-3/4" h, **$75.**

Gilt geometric motif, 1950s-60s, 3-1/2" h, **$25-$35.**

Hobnail pattern, in cobalt, 1960s, marked with conjoined "IG," 3-3/4" h, **$50.**

Iridized blue floral motif, an old Lenox mold, 1970s, 3-1/2" h, **$25+.**

Mount Vernon pattern, an old Cambridge mold, in Amber Glow, 1970s, 3-1/2" h, **$30-$40.**

Mary and Johnny Bull, with labels and marked with con-joined "IG," 1950s, 5-3/4" h, **$75-$100.**

Mount Vernon pattern, an old Cambridge mold, in Verde, 1970s, 3-1/2" h, **$30-$40.**

Old Williamsburg pattern, an old Heisey mold, in Amber Glow, found in other colors, 4" h, **$10+.**

Provincial pattern, an old Heisey mold, in Nut Brown, 1970s, marked with conjoined "IG," 3" h, **$25.**

Sphinx pattern, circa 1900, 3-1/2" h, **$120-$150.**

Spider Web pattern, Soda Gold, 1920s, 3-1/4" h, **$100-$125.**

Vintage pattern, marked with conjoined "IG," 1950s-60s, 4-1/2" h, **$50+** in Milk-glass.

Vintage pattern, marked with conjoined "IG," 1920s, 4-1/2" h, **$75+** in "Rubigold" carnival glass.

Vintage pattern, marked with conjoined "IG," 1920s, 4-1/2" h, **$75+** in amber/amethyst carnival glass.

Vintage pattern, barrel form with pepper grinder, marked with conjoined "IG," also on metal, "The George S. Thompson Corporation – Monterey Park, Calif. USA," 1950s-60s, 3" h without handle, **$65-$75** in Milk-glass.

Waffle pattern, with colored glass tops, found in other colors, 1930s, 2-1/2" h, **$65-$75.**

Zodiac pattern, an old Heisey mold, in Amber Glow, found in other colors, 1970s, marked with label, 3" h, **$30-$35.**

Zodiac pattern, an old Heisey mold, in Verde, found in other colors, 1970s, marked with label, 3" h, **$30-$35.**

INDIANA GLASS CO.

The Indiana Glass Co. began as Beatty-Brady Glass Co. of Dunkirk, Ind., in 1897. It joined the U.S. Glass Co. combine in 1899. The Indiana Glass Co. was established in 1907. In 1983, Lancaster Colony purchased the company, and closed the factory in 2002.

Madrid pattern, 1930s, 4" h, $50+.

Madrid pattern, footed, 1930s, 4-1/4" h, $75-$85.

Tea Room pattern, footed, late 1920s, 4-1/2" h, $95+.

INDIANA TUMBLER AND GOBLET CO.

The Indiana Tumbler and Goblet Co. of Greentown, Ind., operated from 1894 to 1903. The company's wares in chocolate glass and "Holly Amber" are highly prized. The factory was destroyed by fire in 1903. Collectors use the term "Greentown glass" when referring to their products.

Wild Rose and Bow-knot, satin, circa 1900, 3-1/2" h, $75-$85.

JEANNETTE GLASS CO.

The Jeannette (Pa.) Glass Co. was incorporated on June 14, 1898. It started out producing jars for pickles, olives, relishes and mayonnaise. In 1961, the firm bought the McKee Glass Division of Thatcher Glass Manufacturing Co. Jeannette closed in 1983.

Adam pattern, footed, 1932-34, 4" h, **$110+.**

Delphite Basket Weave pattern, marbleized glass in the form of Chianti bottles, late 1930s, 6" h, **$45-$55.**

Cubist pattern, late 1920-30s, 3" h, **$45+.**

Doric pattern, mid- to late 1930s, 3-1/2" h, **$55+.**

Floral pattern, footed, sometimes called Poinsettia, early to mid-1930s, 4" h, **$65+.**

Florigold, footed, 1950s, 4" h, **$65+.**

Hex Optic pattern, late 1920s-early '30s, 3" h, **$45-$55.**

Swirl pattern, mid- to late 1930s, 3-3/4" h, **$60+.**

Sierra pattern, footed, sometimes called Pinwheel, early 1930s, 4" h, **$60+.**

Windsor pattern, 1930s-40s, 3" h, **$60+.**

MT. WASHINGTON

The Mt. Washington Glass Works began operating in 1837 in the Mount Washington area of south Boston. The factory was relocated to New Bedford, Mass., in 1870. From 1880 until 1894, Mt. Washington supplied glass to the Pairpoint Manufacturing Corp. Pairpoint purchased Mt. Washington in 1894. Production of reverse-painted and puffy lampshades continued until about 1915.

Fig form, late 1800s, sold in mixed colors or solid and clear, 2-1/2" h, **$250+.**

Tomato form, hand painted, late 1800s, 2-3/8" diameter, **$250+.**

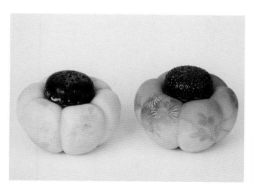

Tomato form, hand painted, late 1800s, 2-3/8" diameter, **$250+.**

Milk-glass with transfer decoration, without caps, late 1800s, possibly Mt. Washington, 2-3/4" h, **$75-$100.**

NEW MARTINSVILLE

The New Martinsville (W.V.) Glass Manufacturing Co. was established in 1901 and became the Viking Glass Co. in 1944. The firm went out of business in 1999.

Janice pattern, 1930s, 3" h, **$95+.**

Rose Relievo pattern, 1902-1907, other opaque colors, 2-1/2" h, **$85-$95.**

Ruby, in 20 Rib pattern, 1925-29, 4-1/4" h, **$90-$100.**

NORTHWOOD

In 1896, Harry Northwood formed the Northwood Co. of Indiana, Pa. In about 1902, he purchased Hobbs, Brockunier & Co. in Wheeling, W.V., and operated two facilities. In 1904, Northwood sold the Pennsylvania plant to its managers. Northwood closed in 1925.

Jeweled Heart pattern, late 1800s, 3" h, $150-$175.

Paneled Sprig pattern, early 1900s, 3-3/4" h, $150-$175.

Reverse S pattern, 1930s, 3-3/8" h, $50+.

PADEN CITY GLASS CO.

Paden City Glass Co. was founded in 1916 in the West Virginia town of the same name. Paden City bought the American Glass Co.'s automated factory in 1949. Both factories closed in 1951.

Party Line pattern, 1930s (?), 3-1/2" h, $75-$100.

Ruby, possibly Paden City, circa 1930s, 3-1/4" h, $75-$85.

RED WING POTTERIES

The commercial production of clay products began in Red Wing, Minn., in 1861. For the next 106 years, products were made by a number of companies, which merged and became known as Red Wing Potteries Inc. Stoneware gave way to art pottery and dinnerware lines in the 1930s. A strike forced the company to close in 1967.

Bobwhite, 1950s-60s, 4-1/4" h and long, **$45-$55.**

Lexington Rose, 1950s, 2-1/2" h and 2-1/4" diameter, **$25+.**

Lute Song, 1950s-60s,
5-1/2" h, **$45+.**

Orleans, 1950s-60s,
2-1/4" h, **$25+.**

Random Harvest,
1950s-60s, 4" and
4-3/4" h, **$45+.**

REGAL CHINA CORP./ROYAL CHINA AND NOVELTY CO.

The Regal China Corp. was founded in Antioch, Ill., in 1938, and was later purchased by the Royal China and Novelty Co. The company made high-quality glazed pottery cookie jars, kitchen canister sets, and salt and pepper shakers. The firm closed in 1992.

Illustrator Ruth Van Tellingen Bendel designed a series of shakers for Regal/Royal in the 1940s in the form of hugging creatures and people. Marks include the name of the figures ("Bear Hug"), "Van Tellingen," "R. Bendel," "Pat Pend," the patent number "2560755," and the style numbers "54-185A" and "158B." The patent was granted on July 15, 1951.

Royal China also decorated the Little Red Riding Hood cookie jars made by the A.E. Hull Pottery Co. of Crooksville, Ohio, but sources differ on which firm actually produced the "go alongs," including the shakers.

R. Bendel Bear Hug in white and brown, found in other color combinations, marked behind "Van Tellingen Bear Hug" with copyright symbol, and "Pat Pend" on the bottom, 1950s to early '60s, 3-3/4" h, **$100+.**

R. Bendel Bunny Hug in white and gray, found in other color combinations, marked behind "B. Bendel Copr. Bunny Hug," and "Pat. 2560755" on the bottom, 1950s to early '60s, 3-3/4" h, **$25-$35.**

R. Bendel Love Bug Huggers in gray-black and pale green, found in other color combinations, marked on back "Bendel Love Bug" and copyright symbol, and on bottom, "Pat No 2560755," 1950s to early '60s, 3-3/4" h, **$65-$75.**

R. Bendel Love Bug Huggers in rust and pale green, found in other color combinations, marked on back "Bendel Love Bug" and copyright symbol, and on bottom, "Pat No 2560755," 1950s to early '60s, 3-1/4" h, **$65-$75.**

R. Bendel Love Bug Huggers in rust and pale green, found in other color combinations, marked on back "Bendel Love Bug" and copyright symbol, and on bottom, "Pat No 2560755," 1950s to early '60s, larger size, 4" h, **$125-$150.**

Van Tellingen Bear Hug in yellow and orange, found in other color combinations, marked behind "Van Tellingen Bear Hug" with copyright symbol, and "Pat Pend" on the bottom, 1950s to early '60s, 3-1/2" h, **$25-$35;** rare in all brown, **$100+.**

Van Tellingen Bear Hug in pink and orange, found in other color combinations, marked behind "Van Tellingen Bear Hug" with copyright symbol, and "Pat Pend" on the bottom, 1950s to early '60s, 3-1/2" h, **$25-$35;** rare in all brown, **$100+.**

Van Tellingen Bear Hug in green and orange, found in other color combinations, marked behind "Van Tellingen Bear Hug" with copyright symbol, and "Pat Pend" on the bottom, 1950s to early '60s, 3-1/2" h, **$25-$35;** rare in all brown, **$100+.**

Van Tellingen Bunny Hug in green and orange, found in other color combinations, marked behind "Van Tellingen Bunny Hug" with copyright symbol, and "Pat Pend" on the bottom, sometimes with "Van Tellingen" in script, 1950s to early '60s, 3-3/4" h, **$25-$35.**

Van Tellingen Bunny Hug in yellow and orange, found in other color combinations, marked behind "Van Tellingen Bunny Hug" with copyright symbol, and "Pat Pend" on the bottom, sometimes with "Van Tellingen" in script, 1950s to early '60s, 3-3/4" h, **$25-$35.**

Van Tellingen Bunny Hug in white and salmon pink, found in other color combinations, marked behind "Van Tellingen Bunny Hug" with copyright symbol, and "Pat Pend" on the bottom, sometimes with "Van Tellingen" in script, 1950s to early '60s, 3-3/4" h, **$25-$35.**

Van Tellingen Mary and White Lamb Huggers, found in other color combinations, marked behind "Van Tellingen" with copyright symbol, and on bottom, "Pat Pend," 1950s to early '60s, 4" and 3-1/2" h, **$65-$75;** rarely found with black lamb, **$100+.**

Van Tellingen Mary and Gray Lamb Huggers, found in other color combinations, marked behind "Van Tellingen" with copyright symbol, and on bottom, "Pat Pend," 1950s to early '60s, 4" and 3-1/2" h, **$65-$75;** rarely found with black lamb, **$100+.**

Van Tellingen Mary and Yellow Lamb Huggers, found in other color combinations, marked behind "Van Tellingen" with copyright symbol, and on bottom, "Pat Pend," 1950s to early '60s, 4" and 3-1/2" h, **$65-$75;** rarely found with black lamb, **$100+.**

Van Tellingen Dutch Huggers, marked behind "Van Tellingen" with copyright symbol, and on bottom, "402," 1950s to early '60s, 3-5/8" h, **$55-$65.**

Van Tellingen Duck Huggers in yellow and black, found in other color combinations, marked below the tails "Van Tellingen" with copyright symbol, bottom unmarked, 1950s to early '60s, 3-1/4" h, **$35-$45**; less for all brown, **$25-$35.**

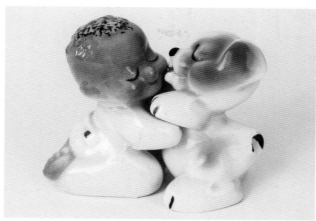

Van Tellingen Boy and Puppy Huggers in brown and white, found in other color combinations, marked on bottom "Van Tellingen" with copyright symbol, 1950s to early '60s, 3-3/4" and 3-5/8" h, **$100+**; rarely found in all black, **$125+.**

Van Tellingen Boy and Puppy Huggers in rust and white, found in other color combinations, marked on bottom "Van Tellingen" with copyright symbol, 1950s to early '60s, 3-3/4" and 3-5/8" h, **$100+**; rarely found in all black, **$125+.**

Van Tellingen Boy and Puppy Huggers in gray-black and white, found in other color combinations, marked on bottom "Van Tellingen" with copyright symbol, 1950s to early '60s, 3-3/4" and 3-5/8" h, **$100+**; rarely found in all black, **$125+.**

Van Tellingen Sailor and Mermaid Huggers, found in other color combinations, marked on Mermaid's tail "Van Tellingen," 1950s to early '60s, 4" h, **$300-$350.**

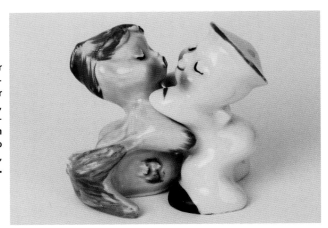

Van Tellingen Sailor and Mermaid Huggers, found in other color combinations, marked on Mermaid's tail "Van Tellingen," 1950s to early '60s, 4" h, **$300-$350.**

Van Tellingen Peek-a-Boo, coordinate with the cookie jar of the same form, marked "Van Tellingen" with copyright symbol, also sometimes found marked on bottom, "Peek a Boo Pat Pend," 1950s to early '60s, 3-1/4" h, **$250-$275.**

Little Red Riding Hood, coordinate with the cookie jar, standard with gold trim, largest of three sizes, unmarked, 5-1/2" h, **$200-$225**; rarely found in medium size, about 4-1/2" h, no established value.

Little Red Riding Hood, coordinate with the cookie jar, standard with gold trim, smallest of three sizes, unmarked, 3-1/2" h, **$75-$85**; rarely found in medium size, about 4-1/2" h, no established price.

ROSEMEADE

The Wahpeton (N.D.) Pottery Co. was formed in 1940 by businessman Robert J. Hughes and Laura Taylor, a potter trained at the University of North Dakota. The two were married in 1943. Taylor was born in Rosemeade Township, Ransom County, N.D., and named the pottery after her birthplace. Pheasants in many variations were probably the most popular Rosemeade item, with at least 19 different designs known. Laura Taylor Hughes died of cancer in 1959. Production continued until 1961 and the salesroom remained open until 1964.

Black bears, male and female, with foil label, 3-1/3 and 2-3/4" h, **$85-$100.**

Brown bears, males, with foil label, 3-1/3" h, **$65-$75.**

Siamese cats, red, with foil label and decal, "Badlands, S.D.," 3-1/2 h, **$85-$100.**

Siamese cats, brown and tan, with foil label, 2-7/8" h, **$85-$100.**

Chow Chow heads, with breed label, 2-1/8" h, **$60-$70.**

Fox terriers, with foil label, and with breed label, 2-1/4" h, **$45-$50.**

Puppies, with foil label, 3" h, **$85-$95.**

Colts, with foil labels, found in other colors, 2-1/2" and 3" long, **$80-$90.**

Fish, with foil label and marked "Rose-meade No. Dak." in script, found in other colors, 2 3/4" h, **$75-$85.**

Jack rabbits, with foil label, 2-3/4" long, **$115-$125.**

Kangaroos, with foil label, also ink-stamped "Rose-meade" in script on the bottom, 3" h, **$85-$100.**

Mice, unmarked (same figures also found without holes and on ash-trays), 1-3/4" h and long, **$35-$50.**

Mule heads, unmarked, 3-1/2" long, **$70-$80.**

Skunks, medium size, with foil label, same form also found as figurine, 3" long, **$55-$65.**

Skunks, larger size, with foil label, same form also found as figurine, 3-1/2" long, **$65-$75.**

Turkeys, unmarked, 2-7/8 and 3" h, **$85-$100.**

Tropical fish, unmarked or with foil label, 2-3/4" h, **$85-$100.**

Brook trout, with foil label, 5" long, **$225-$250**; rarely found with molded name on tail, price doubles.

Ducklings, found in several colors, unmarked or with foil label, 2-3/4" h, **$80-$100** pair.

Ducklings, with foil labels, 3" long, if perfect, **$80-$100**.

Mallard drake and hen, unmarked, 2 and 3-3/4" h, **$85-$100**.

Bantam hen and rooster, unmarked, 3-1/2 and 2-3/4" h, **$95-$105.**

Rooster and hen, unmarked, 3-1/4 and 2-1/8" h, **$70-$85.**

Pelicans, with foil label, 3" h, **$90-$110.**

Pheasants (tails down), unmarked or with foil label, 4-1/2" long, **$80-$100.**

Pheasants (tails
up), unmarked
or with foil label,
3-1/2 and
2-1/2" h,
$50-$60.

Bobwhite quail,
unmarked,
2-3/4 and
1-3/4" h,
$65-$75.

Western quail,
unmarked, 2-1/2
and 2-3/8" h,
$120-$130.

Swans,
unmarked,
2-1/3" h,
$85-$100.

Blue tulip buds,
with foil label,
2" h, **$50-$60.**

Brussels sprouts,
unmarked,
1-3/4" h,
$60-$75.

Corncobs,
unmarked,
2-1/8" h,
$45-$50.

Cucumbers,
unmarked,
2-1/2" long,
$60-$75.

SHAWNEE POTTERY

Shawnee Pottery was founded in Zanesville, Ohio, in 1937. In addition to vases, novelty ware, flowerpots, planters, lamps and cookie jars, the firm made three dinnerware lines: Corn, Lobster Ware and Valencia. The company went out of business in 1961.

Baluster-form "Decorator" style, unmarked, late 1940s to early '50s, 3-1/2" h, **$35-$40.**

Bashful ducklings, unmarked, late 1940s to early '50s, 3-1/4" h, **$50-$55.**

Chefs, unmarked, late 1940s to early '50s, 3-1/2" h, **$35-$40.**

Chefs with gold trim, unmarked, late 1940s to early '50s, 3-1/2" h, **$55-$60.**

Cooky and Happy, coordinate with the cookie jars, unmarked, late 1940s to early '50s, 5-1/4" h, **$85-$95.** Note that Cooky has her hands behind her back, but on the cookie jar her hands are in front.

Corncobs, smaller size, unmarked, late 1940s to early '50s, 3-3/8" h, **$40-$45.**

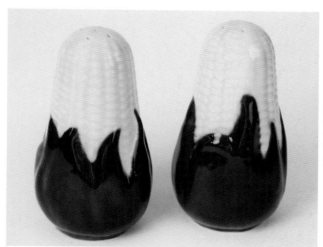

Corncobs, larger kitchen size, unmarked, late 1940s to early '50s, 5-1/2" h, **$55-$60.**

Corncobs, some-times called Maize when found in white, larger kitchen size, unmarked, late 1940s to early '50s, 5-1/4" h, **$55-$60.**

Children, smaller size, unmarked, late 1940s to early '50s, 3-3/8" h, **$40-$50.**

Dutch children, larger size, marked "USA 323S and 323P," 5" and 4-3/4" h, **$75-$85.**

Dutch children with gold trim, larger size, marked "USA 323S and 323P," 5" and 4-3/4" h, **$85-$95.**

Dutch children, larger size, marked "USA 323S and 323P," 5" and 4-3/4" h, **$75-$85.**

Farmer pigs, unmarked, late 1940s to early '50s, 3-1/2" h, **$45-$50.**

Flowerpots, unmarked, late 1940s to early '50s, 3-1/2" h, **$35-$40**; add **$10** for gold trim.

Flowers, unmarked, late 1940s to early '50s, 3-1/2" w, **$55-$60.**

Fruit, smaller size, marked "USA 82," and faint ink stamp, 2-3/4" h, **$45-$50.**

Fruit, larger size, marked "USA 8," and faint ink stamp, 4" h, **$55-$65.**

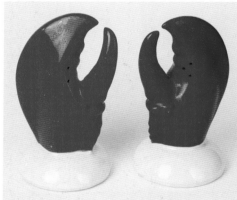

Lobster claws, marked "USA," late 1940s to early '50s, 5" h, **$100-$125.**

Milk cans, unmarked, late 1940s to early '50s, 3-1/2" h, **$35-$40.**

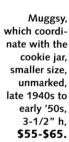

Muggsy, which coordinate with the cookie jar, smaller size, unmarked, late 1940s to early '50s, 3-1/2" h, **$55-$65.**

Puss N Boots, coordinate with the cookie jar, not known in a larger size, unmarked, late 1940s to early '50s, 3-1/2" h, **$55-$65.**

Roosters, smaller size, unmarked, late 1940s to early '50s, 3-3/8" h, **$35-$40.**

Roosters, larger size, unmarked, late 1940s to early '50s, 5-1/4" h, **$65-$70.**

Smiley, coordinate with the cookie jar, found in many variations, rare in these colors, may have been repainted or a lunch-hour project, unmarked, late 1940s to early '50s, 3-3/8" h, **$65-$75.**

Smiley and Winnie, coordinate with the cookie jars, smaller size, found in many variations, unmarked, late 1940s to early '50s, 3-3/8" h, **$50-$75** depending on decoration detail.

Smiley and Winnie, coordinate with the cookie jars, larger size, found in many variations, unmarked, late 1940s to early '50s, 5-3/8" h, **$100-$125** depending on decoration detail.

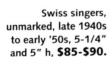

Swiss singers, unmarked, late 1940s to early '50s, 5-1/4" and 5" h, **$85-$90.**

Watering cans, unmarked, late 1940s to early '50s, 2-3/8" h, **$35-$40.**

Wheelbarrows, unmarked, late 1940s to early '50s, 2-1/4" h, **$35-$40.**

Winking owls, with gold trim, coordinate with the cookie jar, not known in a larger size, unmarked, late 1940s to early '50s, 3-3/8" h, **$75-$85.**

Winking owls, coordinate with the cookie jar, unmarked, late 1940s to early '50s, 3-3/8" h, **$35-$45.**

Winking owls, coordinate with the cookie jar, unmarked, late 1940s to early '50s, 3-3/8" h, **$35-$45.**

SMITH GLASS CO.

In 1907, Lewis E. Smith of Mount Pleasant, Pa., made his own mustard and started a company to make glass containers. Smith produced items in the "Moon and Stars" and "Daisy and Button" patterns. The firm is still in business.

Snake Dance pattern, 1920s, only made in black, 3-1/2" h, **$175-$200.**

TIFFIN GLASS

A. J. Beatty & Sons glass factory of Steubenville, Ohio, relocated to Tiffin, Ohio, in 1888. Beatty & Sons merged with the U.S. Glass Co. combine in 1892. In 1938, the offices of the U.S. Glass Co. were transferred from Pittsburgh to Tiffin. The firm purchased Duncan & Miller molds in 1955. Four employees bought the plant and renamed it Tiffin Art Glass Co. in 1963. The company closed in 1980.

Footed shakers in satin glass with hand painting, sold in mixed colors, 1920s, 3-1/2" h, **$65-$75.**

U.S. GLASS CO.

This was a consolidation of 19 companies established in 1891 and based in Pittsburgh. The conglomerate reorganized the industry, calling the companies "Factory A, D, M, O, R," etc. Firms included Beatty, Bellaire, Block Light, Bryce, Central, Challinor Taylor, Duncan & Miller, Gillinder, Hobbs Brockunier & Co., King and O'Hara. The group went into receivership in 1907, but many firms continued to produce wares independently for decades after.

California pattern, dark amethyst, circa 1900, 3" h with finial, **$120-$130.**

VIKING GLASS CO.

The New Martinsville (W.V.) Glass Manufacturing Co. was established in 1901 and became the Viking Glass Co. in 1944. The firm went out of business in 1999.

Amethyst floral motif, an old New Martinsville mold, early 1960s, 3-3/4" h, **$25+.**

Bull's Eye pattern in ruby, 1970s, 4-3/4" h, **$85-$95.**

Georgian pattern, late 1980s, 5" h, **$55-$65.**

Marigold floral motif, an old New Martinsville mold, early 1960s, 3-3/4" h, **$25+.**

WESTMORELAND GLASS CO.

The Westmoreland Glass Co. of Grapeville, Pa., was established in 1889 by a group operating the Specialty Glass Co. in East Liverpool, Ohio. The firm closed in 1984.

American Hobnail pattern, Brandywine Blue opalescent, footed, 1971, unmarked or with conjoined "WG," 4-1/2" h, **$75-$100.**

American Hobnail pattern, Candlelight opalescent, footed, 1970s, unmarked or with conjoined "WG," 4-1/2" h, **$50-$60.**

American Hobnail pattern, Lilac opalescent, footed, 1983-84, unmarked or with conjoined "WG," 4-1/2" h, no established value.

Beaded Edge pattern, Milk-glass, footed,
1950s, unmarked, 4-1/2" h, **$35**; if decorated,
$50-$75.

Beaded Grape pattern, Milk-glass, footed,
1960s, unmarked or with conjoined "WG," 5" h,
$35-$40.

Della Robbia pattern, footed, stained, 1930s-
70s, unmarked or with conjoined "WG," 5" h,
$75-$85.

Della Robbia pattern, Milk-glass, footed, 1950s-
60s, unmarked or with conjoined "WG," 5" h,
$45-$50.

English Hobnail pattern, green, footed, 1930s, 4-1/4" h, **$50-$65.**

English Hobnail pattern, in crystal and ebony, round-footed, with handled tray; unmarked or with conjoined "WG," shakers 4-5/8" h, tray 5-3/4" h, **$100+** set.

English Hobnail pattern, barrel form with pepper grinder, unmarked or with conjoined "WG," also marked on metal, "The George Thompson Corporation – Los Angeles – Patent Applied For," 1950s-60s, 3-1/4" h without handle, **$40-$45** in Milkglass.

English Hobnail pattern, Ruby, footed, 1940s, unmarked or with conjoined "WG," 4-5/8" h, **$85-$95.**

English Hobnail pattern, crystal and ebony (with ebony base, 1929-31), round-footed, unmarked or with conjoined "WG," 4-5/8" h, **$75-$85.**

English Hobnail pattern, Amber Stained, round-footed, 1960s, unmarked or with conjoined "WG," 4-5/8" h, **$55-$65.**

English Hobnail pattern, crystal and ebony (with ebony base, 1929-31), square-footed, unmarked or with conjoined "WG," 4-5/8" h, **$75-$85.**

English Hobnail pattern, crystal, square-footed, introduced 1920s and made for 65 years, unmarked or with conjoined "WG," 4-5/8" h, **$25-$35.**

Lotus pattern, green (also known in pink), footed, 1930s-40s, unmarked or with conjoined "WG," 4-5/8" h, **$85-$95.**

Old Quilt pattern, Milk-glass, 1950s-60s, unmarked or with conjoined "WG," 3-1/2" h, **$30-$35.**

Old Quilt pattern, Ice Blue carnival glass, late 1970s, unmarked or with conjoined "WG," 3-1/2" h, **$55-$65.**

Paneled Grape pattern, blown, Milk-glass, 1950s-60s, unmarked or with conjoined "WG," 4-1/4" h, **$75-$85.**

Paneled Grape variant, Milk-glass, footed, 1950s-60s, unmarked or with conjoined "WG," 4-7/8" h, **$25.**

Paneled Grape variant, Brandywine Blue, footed, 1940s-1985, unmarked or with conjoined "WG," 4-7/8" h, **$50-$60.**

Pansy pattern, hand painted (scarce), 1969-76, unmarked or with conjoined "WG," 4-1/2" h, **$100-$125.**

Pansy pattern, 1969-76, in amber, unmarked or with conjoined "WG," 4-1/2" h, **$60-$70.**

Pansy pattern, in ice-blue carnival glass, 1969-76, unmarked or with conjoined "WG," 4-1/2" h, **$75+.**

Princess Feather pattern, crystal, footed, 1930s-50s, unmarked or with conjoined "WG," 4-5/8" h, **$35.**

Princess Feather pattern, Golden Sunset, footed, 1960s, unmarked or with conjoined "WG," 4-5/8" h, **$50+.**

Thousand Eyes pattern, with stain, footed, 1934-50, unmarked or with conjoined "WG," 4-1/2" h, **$75-$85.**

Thousand Eyes pattern, crystal without stain, footed, 1934-50, unmarked or with conjoined "WG," 4-1/2" h, **$40.**

UNKNOWN MAKER, PATTERNS

"15 Swirl" pattern, multicolor cased glass, late 1800s, 3" h, **$200-$225.**

Beaded Scroll pattern, early 1900s, 3-1/4" h, **$45-$55.**

Classic green kitchen shakers with applied labels, made by several companies, 1940s, 5" h, **$50.**

Crackle-glass, showing color variation, with two-piece caps, circa 1900, 4-1/4" h, **$75-$100.**

Crystal in an unknown pattern, 1920s, 2-3/4" h, **$35-$45.**

Crystal in an unknown pattern, 1920s, 2-3/4" h, **$35-$45.**

Crystal in an unknown pattern, 1920s, 3" h, **$35-$45.**

Crystal in a fancy-arch pattern, 1920s, 3-1/2" h, **$35-$45.**

Crystal in an unknown pattern, with No. 1 sanitary caps, 1920s, possibly Heisey, 3-1/2" h, **$45-$55.**

Georgian pattern, 4" h, **$45-$55.**

Kitchen shakers, with pea, corn and pepper decoration, 1950s, impressed mark USA 24, possibly Hull, 3-3/4" h, **$25-$35.**

Opalescent dot-optic pattern, attributed to Hobbs, Brockunier & Co., late 1800s, 3-1/4" h, **$75-$100.**

Nippon, with hand-painted landscapes, circa 1900, marked, 3-1/4" h, **$75-$100.**

Pansy variation, in Milk-glass, age unknown, unmarked, 4-1/4" h, **$65+.**

Ruby flash souvenir, Louisville, Ky., 1909, in a fancy-arch pattern, 3-1/8" h, **$75-$100.**

Satin-glass, footed, with acid-etch rose pattern, 1930s (?), 4-1/4" h, **$75.**

Square ruby,
1-1/2" square,
$45-$55.

Wrinkled Panel
pattern,
early 1900s, 3" h,
$55-$65.

Zipper pattern,
1920s, 2-/4" h,
$35-$45.

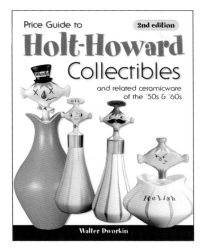

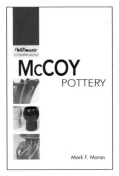